Selling Backwards

HOW TO SELL MORE ADS TO DIGITALLY
FOCUSED, SOCIAL MEDIA SATURATED,
SERIOUSLY CONFUSED
ADVERTISERS.

Ryan R. Dohrn

360AdSales.com
Brain Swell Media LLC

Brain Swell Media LLC
P.O. Box 403
Jackson, SC 29831
www.SellingBackwards.com
www.BrainSwellMedia.com
www.360AdSales.com

Selling Backwards/ Ryan R Dohrn. —1st ed.
ISBN 978-1-4951-1229-4

Contents

To Andre', Dylan and Ethan. Your support is unwavering.

Also, many thanks to NanC and Diana for your help in making this book a reality.

A dramatic change or else.

I n 2009 my sales coaching clients were struggling to sell anything. I mean *anything*. The "Great Recession" had brought nearly every sales organization to its knees. The methods we had used in the past were no longer working. Despite budget cutbacks we hit the road hard armed with a top-notch presentation filled with deep values and deep discounts. As we sat in front of a longtime client, they put the final nail in the coffin when they said they loved us, our fresh ideas and our marketing products, but they were not renewing their advertising because they needed money to pay their staff. Wow! How do you handle that sales objection? I decided to look back to draw on my years with serious sales-driven organizations like The NY Times Company and Disney. Perhaps my sales coaching clients could somehow better market their products? Maybe they just needed to hit the road even harder? Perhaps we needed to really discount? Maybe we needed to raise prices? At one point one of my magazine clients offered free ads and not one client would bite! No matter what we tried, nothing was moving the sales needle upward. Sure, they had some business, but not enough to pay the bills long-term or keep all the promises they were making. This made me realize that the recession was changing everything. I needed a new angle. I needed a new sales approach. My successful sales and marketing methods of the past were just not enough any more. I asked my sales coaching clients to stick with me and I promised I would find an answer to this dilemma that was sweeping the nation.

I began my search for a new and better way to sell. I went online and watched sales training courses and found little help. Surely someone out there had an answer to this national sales dilemma. I attended conferences and found little help there either. I looked to the best of the best in the sales training business and found the same tired answers and techniques. I thought I would fall over dead if one more "sales expert" told me to "....*work smarter and not harder.*" As I sat in my office during that turbulent time, I thought back to my earliest years and really dug deep, searching for answers. I had looked forward for help unsuccessfully, so now I tried looking back-wards instead. I mean waaaaay back. It didn't take me to long, once I changed my direction of thought, to find the answer I was seeking. Often, when things are not going in the right di-rection you need to look at things from a completely different perspective. At first I resisted. I had been taught to not look back. To always fail forward. Come on, I have been in the sales and marketing business for nearly 20 years! I was just pushing forward hoping that by working harder, it would all be ok. I had thousands of ideas a week for my clients. The failure be-fore me was not about a lack of ideas. Advertisers were just not willing to bet even one penny on a new idea. They had lost faith. They lacked confidence. They were just not going to take any risks on a new idea. They were in survival mode. I finally gave in and realized that I had no choice, I had to look backwards to find the answer. Not only did I find the answer to my sales dilemma, I found a new direction in my sales career. I found the answer that changed my life and the lives of the thousands of sales people looking to me for help.

Growing up on a farm in Eastern Iowa, we built fences to contain our horses, cows and pigs. Building a fence is not for the faint of heart. It requires a ton of time and effort. A well-built fence will last for many years, while a poorly built fence will fall over. And, if an animal becomes entangled in a poorly built fence, they can be seriously injured or even killed. One part of the fence building process is installing fence posts to create a straight line on which you will hang your fence, either wire or boards. As a child I would work hard, digging the fence post holes and lining them up in a "perfect" line with my eye. I would stand right over the top of the previous hole, look down the line for the next spot and dig the next hole. I was truly proud of my work. My slightly amused father, observing my work from a distance, saw his young son building a crooked fence. He then asked me to step back from the fence post line about 10 feet. At that moment, from a distance, I could actually see how badly misaligned my holes were, which resulted in a crooked fence. (Perhaps you have had the same thing happen while hanging a picture on the wall?)

This lesson from my youth gave me the answer to my sales dilemma. It was right in front of me the whole the time. I just needed to step back to see how crooked or far off base I really was. My sales process was out of alignment. I was working hard. I was digging away at my prospect list. I was trying to build a strong client base. But, the results were sub-par at best. In my sales life, I needed to take a big step back, realizing that the world around me had changed dramatically; I I needed to develop a new sales process.

Because of the global economic crisis, business owners were no longer taking any risks. Sales prospects that would have jumped at an idea two years ago were scared to death. So, I needed a new sales process or my customers and I would simply not survive. I needed to flip my sales process on its head, start from scratch and do things completely different than I had been doing for years. I was going to have to attack this issue by starting from the exact opposite side of the issue. I then realized that we all needed to start by first taking a giant step backwards. We needed to start *Selling Backwards.*

I use this fence story on a regular basis with the sales clients I coach. I believe it illustrates how sales executives often miss the bigger picture because they live in a "bubble" or "in the moment." They often need to really step back to see how their sales process is misaligned. I work with veteran sales people on a daily basis that keep their nose down to the grindstone, working in the same way, but just can't seem to find ultimate sales success. They often tell me that they can "sell themselves" out of a bad spot. These sales people do not see that a completely different sales approach is required now to close the deal.

I have had the privilege of teaching, coaching and mentoring sales people around the world. From Abilene to Australia I have witnessed sales people's careers literally transformed by making the small tweaks I have suggested to their overall sales process. Many were a part of my media ad sales focus. Many were not. In my opinion, having a quality sales process is critical to whatever you sell. My primary focus has been the marketing and selling of advertising for media companies and the Internet. But that is just a product not a path. Having a quality sales process is truly not industry specific. Sure, each industry has subtle differences, but what I have discovered is that true sales success comes from developing and executing on a sales process filled with repeatable patterns of success. A good sales process is dependent on only one thing... you! Your success in sales is truly dependent on your ability to execute and implement my techniques in your sales world. Your success will be further enhanced by your ability to find repeatable patterns of success. Here's the lesson: If you have no sales process, it is literally impossible to learn where you excel or fail.

A great student will learn from a variety of teachers. Often those teachers can be experts beyond their industry or focus. This is exactly why a great football coach like former Indian-

SELLING BACKWARDS • 11

apolis Colts head coach Tony Dungy can offer advice to Fortune 500 CEOs, for example. As a sales coach, sales success stories flow into my office. I am never surprised when a non-advertising sales executive raves of his success using the *Selling Backwards* system. You see, its not about "the system", it's about your ability to *implement* the system.

It is important to point out that the sales environment of today is so much different than the days of *Tommy Boy* or *Glengarry Glen Ross*. In the 1980's and 1990's, sales people were information providers to their clients. They were the single conduit by which prospects learned about new and emerging products and services. Now, thanks to the Internet, the role of the sales person has changed dramatically.

We now live in a world where people have more access to information than ever before. Most sales prospects don't even think they need you. They have the Internet to research new products and services. Whether you are selling used cars, software or local magazine advertising, you first need to fix your sales process and eliminate random patterns. Next you need to focus on the client and fix their problems. Lastly, become the client's hero and work every day to stay in hero status.

My goal is to provide you with concrete answers and examples, and to share only what really works. I do not teach
theory or give pie-in-the sky ideas. I have hundreds of examples of sales people who have improved their personal sales by
following my simple yet effective approach to selling more effectively every day. The real question is whether you are ready
to adopt a new media sales process and execute that process
every day.

Rex and Julie sat in an ad sales workshop I was teaching for
two days. At the end of day one I could see that my message
was not resonating with either of these two sales people. At
face value it seemed that their ego was just too large, prevent-
ing them from learning. (An interesting point to note here,
both of these sales reps had not made goal in the last 3
months.) So, I decided to dig deeper. I asked them why they
were so reluctant to try what I was teaching. Their answer, "*It
sounds like a lot of work. We want to work smarter and not
harder.*" It's not a choice, you have to work harder AND
smarter. Selling advertising is not any easy job. If it were, everyone would be doing it! Plus, if you want to be a raging sales
success, you will certainly need to work harder, but my methods will allow you to be smarter about the hard work you are
putting in every day. I can share the *Selling Backwards Sales*

SELLING BACKWARDS • 13

System and its methods with anyone. The success lies in YOU and what you do with what you learn. Execution will be your Achilles heel. Execution should be your goal. Execution separates the good from the great.

As for Rex and Julie... both grew their personal sales by 20% in less than three months. Is their success with the *Selling Backwards Sales System* typical? Yes it is. Can you do this as well? Yes you can.

CHAPTER ONE

What does selling backwards mean?

For most of us, *selling backwards* begins at a very young age and we don't even realize it. At the age of 9, my son Dylan wanted to go to the lake to swim and play. We live about 45 miles from the lake, so it's not just a drop-what-you're-doing-and-run-over-there-quickly type of proposition. Add to that distance another child, a wife that has errands to run and this trip requires a bit of planning, several decisions and a parental desire to go. It was a Tuesday when Dylan first asked and I said no. We were committed to other things. The timing was just not good, etc. Sound like your recent sales life? Dylan was rejected. He left to return on Wednesday with a different approach. "Dad you sure do travel a lot and we would all like to spend some time with you on Saturday at the lake." I gave in and said that on Saturday we would go to the lake. First thing

Saturday morning, Dylan was in my ear ready to go to the lake.
I put him off with some last minute work I needed to do. He
was back in an hour. *"Ready yet? Come on dad you promised."*
I had not made a "promise;" more like a subtle commitment to
go. I told Dylan that after lunch we would go because the water would be warmer then. To be honest, I just wanted to sit
around all day and watch a movie and relax. The idea of nearly
2 hours in the car and four hours in the sun was not my idea of
fun that day. At lunchtime, Dylan showed up with his swimsuit
on, goggles and a towel. *"Ready yet? Come on dad, you need
to get outside. You worked hard all week. You need to relax on
the water. You said that you loved the lake. Let's not sit
around all day."* Hmmm. I wonder where he learned that bit
of persuasion? I looked at the weather online and there was a
small chance of showers. I told Dylan to give me another hour
to see what the weather looks like, and perhaps we would go
then. I assumed that he would give up at some point and get
engrossed in a video game or something. An hour later, he was
back. Wow, this kid would just not give up. *"Ready to go yet?
Come on dad. Billy is at the lake and said the water is great."* I
put him off one final time, hoping that he'd finally just give up.
Not a chance. An hour later Dylan moves in to close the deal.
"You know Dad, Tommy's dad does this to him too. Makes

promises and then puts him off. Tommy's dad is a real..." Fine. I give in. Let's go!

The best sales people in the world are under the age of 10. Let's admit it, kids are excellent at getting what they want. They know exactly what buttons to press to get the situation to move in their direction. They are masters at learning what makes their parents tick. They use every little trick in the book, plus they apply a level of persistence that is unwavering. But, it was not just the persistence that moved the needle. It was the whole process. Just like most sales people, Dylan first tried to pitch his proposition. That method failed. So, he sold me by selling the idea of going to the lake completely backwards.

First it was a request for a commitment. Then, it was Dylan trying to hold me to that commitment. Then he added pressure by knowing my desires and true goals. And then he was back with more pressure and the "bad dad" closed the deal! If we only focused on the persistence in this story, then we would have missed the process. The real learning moment in all of this is if Dylan realizes he has found a process and potential repeatable pattern of success. If he tries this approach again and it works, he has a sales process for life.

With the *Selling Backwards Sales System* we are looking to create the best sales process filled with repeatable patterns of success. It is critical that you understand this point... we are looking to create the best sales process filled with <u>repeatable patterns of success</u>. Rather than pitching the features, advantages and benefits of our offering to a client, we start by understanding deeply what makes that client tick. We get their commitment or desire to want business success. We then remove risk by sharing with them success stories of other clients that are happy. We seek to understand their needs, asking great questions that others are not asking, before we pitch. We close the deal by again focusing on the clients desire to see success through the purchase. Then, we work to retain them as a client for life.

Today more than ever before, clients are self-focused. If you want to win, your sales process has to be all about THEM and very little about YOU or your product. You need to sell it backwards. You need to start with them. You need to create an "all about the Client proposition." You need to understand and build on their self-centeredness for success.

When we are able to ask great questions and learn what makes the client tick, we are one step closer to creating a solution they actually want and need, and one that we can actually propose and close. Rather than pitching a product that a client may not be ready or willing to buy, we identify their needs, goals and desires and provide solutions that exceed those desires. To do this, we need to understand which buttons to press and what makes them tick. We need to redirect our efforts and make the client front and center. We need to start with THEM. So, lets flip the age-old model of presenting the perfect pitch on its head and look at the sales process completely backwards. What if I said there is no such thing as a sales pitch anymore? Let me be clear, there is no such thing as a sales pitch anymore!

If our end game is to have a successful client for life, then having the perfect, predictable slide deck, demo or media kit up front is not the answer. That sales model will never get you the full results you need in order to be a sales superstar. Think about it, coming to a sales call with a prepared Power Point presentation or a generic media kit means you are in "presenting mode." That is a YOU focused proposition. Instead, let's go at it backwards. Start by sharing about the success of others just like your client who have used your product or service. Rather than pitching a product or service and seeing what sticks, let's start by fully understanding the client's points of pain, points of desire and points of hope.

Let's focus on their desire for business success. Then, let's marry each thing we have to offer with a success story to boost customer morale and confidence. Let's ask great questions that lead to better understanding, rather than standard questions asked by others in our field. Let's be resource-focused sales people that offer more than what we are there to sell. Perhaps we only present our product as the last part of the total sales process, as if what we have to offer is the key ingredient to success. Let's flip your sales process on its head and let's master the new sales process of *Selling Backwards*.

I've been in the sales and marketing business since 1994. Over the years I have found that there are four pillars to sales success. I like to call them my four "P's" of sales success.

1. People
2. Product
3. Price
4. Process

The first "P" is for People. In his book, *Good to Great,* Jim Collins refers to having "...the right people on the bus." As a manager, ask yourself if you have the right people on your team to get the job done. If you're an individual sales rep, ask yourself if you're up for the challenge. Do you have what it takes to succeed in sales?

The second "P" is for Product. Do you have a good product? Let me be clear, you do not have to have the number one product on the market to be a success. It is more about your belief in your product. For hundreds of years, sales people have fought it out in a marketplace of competing products. Just keep in mind, and we will discuss more later, you must always fight to show why your product will better solve a client's problems or better meet their needs. That is called your differentiating factor. The price becomes the deciding factor when products look or sound similar. People will pay more for something when and only when they understand the full value of the product to them.

The next "P" is for Price. So, where are you on price? You can't imagine the number of times while consulting with a client, I'll discover the nearest competitors are priced thousands of dollars less expensive; or even thousands of dollars *more* expensive than the nearest competitors. You simply must consider the entire market when evaluating your pricing structure. If your product is not priced competitively, you'll likely have difficulty with the complete sales process.

The last "P" is for Process, and is one of the most important in my opinion. In the last several years of consulting with various media companies, I have traveled the United

States extensively and have also coached sales people for companies in Germany, Spain, Holland, New Zealand, Australia and the United Kingdom. Regardless of the location, I have discovered that companies typically have good people, adequate products and accurate pricing. However, almost without exception, their process (or lack thereof) is their Achilles' heel. Sometimes companies will have a sales process but it will be poorly defined and not managed well. More often than not, I have observed that companies simply have no sales process at all. They have no process for prospecting new customers. They have no process for dealing with what I call "in-progress" customers. They have no retention process for retaining the current client base. It reminds me of a person driving a car with half full tires while complaining about bad gas mileage! The problem is usually very evident, but they refuse to add air to fix the issue. They have become so used to the bad situation that is seems "normal."

As you might expect, companies without definable, executable sales processes are companies that are missing out on thousands and thousands of revenue dollars. That's why I focus on the sales PROCESS when I do consulting, coaching and speaking engagements. Having a good process will prevent an organization from being hindered by randomness. Plus, a process allows you to identify repeatable patterns of success. No process means success is a random occurrence.

Randomness means different things in various fields but typically, it means having a lack of pattern or predictability in events. Some of the "symptoms" for randomness include haphazardness, arbitrariness, casualness, uncertainty and finally – chance. Doesn't sound like a very organized and intelligent way to go about exceeding your monthly sales quota, does it? In fact, in the sales profession, randomness will kill you. It will often increase your stress by forcing you to sell, sell, and sell right up to the final, last-second deadline.

Randomness causes you to lose hundreds of hours a year because you don't have a detailed and organized process for success. And finally, randomness will drastically slow any upward mobility you hope to achieve in your sales career because without a process, you cannot repeat what works. You have no way to track what has worked.

As I observe the habits of sales professionals, it looks to me like a bad game of darts. Let's just throw a few and see where they hit. There is a reason why Henry Ford used an assembly line process to grow his business. Sure, a group of qualified people could build a car without an assembly line. But to increase productivity and identify where problems occurred, a process was the answer to success. No manager in their right mind wants someone who randomly handles the accounts, who views the job responsibilities casually, and who drifts through the day and weeks with no real plan or process. The superstars in sales organizations are easy to spot. They operate at 155 mph and leave a pretty big mess behind them. Why? They have identified a process and they are rolling forward like a freight train. They have no time for the little details. Can this be a problem? Of course. But, taking this "A" player to superstar status is more about perfecting their process than trying to improve their housekeeping habit.. Keep in mind, no matter what wake they leave behind them, most arrive early, stay late, and they do whatever is necessary to get their jobs done. It's about teaching them to eliminate any randomness and perfect their process.

Here's a great example of a superstar who used a repeatable pattern for success. Everyone can agree that Michael Jordan is one of the best basketball players of all time. He had tremendous natural ability and talent, and was a gifted athlete from a young age. But, so are a lot of other basketball players. So what made him different? Michael became a legend because of his work ethic, shooting hundreds of free throws during practice sessions each week, and working on other mental aspects of his game in the off-season. Michael was a highly disciplined individual who was never satisfied with just 'good enough.' Randomness was not a problem with Michael Jordan, and I guarantee he had a lot of repeatable patterns of success as a part of his total process.

Stopping your randomness is not difficult, but it requires discipline. To help you fight randomness at every corner, you might want to place a yellow sticky note on your computer screen that says, "STOP BEING RANDOM." I'm serious. Focus on your process if you want to be a raging superstar of sales success.

IMPORTANT NOTE: This book is about the fourth "P" which is process. By nature I am not a "process" kind of guy. I am a creative person who does not particularly like an agenda or to-do list. But I have seen success in my sales life be refining my process to a shareable pattern that you are reading today.

So, what is the *Selling Backwards Sales Process*? There are five very distinct steps.

1. Gaining access/new business development
2. Hosting great sales calls
3. Presenting great proposals
4. Excellent follow-up

5. Customer retention

Step one is undoubtedly the most difficult, and that is "gaining access" or "prospecting." What are the things you need to do in order to get through that door to a meeting with the client? How can you effectively get past the gatekeeper to get a meeting with a decision-maker?

Step two is "hosting great sales calls." What can you do to remove risk and increase the customer's interest? What questions can you ask that will make the most effective use of your time and that of your client's?

Step three is "presenting proposals." I believe this step is the easiest step to accomplish in my sale process and in fact, I often include a proposal when making a sales call, which saves time for me and better yet, saves time for my client.

Step four is "follow-up." I consult with media firms all over the country and constantly talk to sales professionals who tell me they are good at following up after their sales calls. I have seen them in action, and I beg to differ. Having an excellent (not just adequate) follow-up technique is absolutely critical to closing sales.

The fifth and final step in my sales process is "retention." What actions are you going to take in order to retain your customers? I think you would agree that retention is much cheaper than acquisition. Yet, most companies do not have a retention plan at all.

I'm going to break down each of these steps into more depth because I think it's so incredibly important. Please note that the steps contained within each of these five areas of focus are designed to be easy to follow and understand. The *Selling Backwards Sale System* is a total process. Just like a chocolate chip cookie recipe, you truly should not skip steps. My goal in writing this book was to present you a clear guide to sales success. A great guide will map out each step of the process journey. I promise to be a great guide.

CHAPTER 2

---

5 steps, The critical pieces of the Selling Backwards Sales Process.

T his chapter will serve as a mission briefing for our journey.
I will provide to you an overview of the five steps to my
Selling Backwards Sales Process. Then in each subsequent
chapter, I will explain each step in further detail. As a sales
professional that has read hundreds of business books myself, I
like to get a 50,000-foot view of a program before getting
thrown into the weeds. I hope you agree. If you are using this
book as a training tool for your team, this overview will help
your team wrap their heads around the total concept without
having all the specific details up front. Please keep in mind that
reading only this overview and then running out on the street
to sell is not advised. Doing so would be like watching a video

about swimming, and then jumping off the diving board into the deep end of the pool, hoping that you could survive without really knowing how to swim. There is a ton of detail for each step if you want to reach your full potential as a sales person.

Now, before we get into the five steps of my sales process, let me be clear on something. During the *Selling Backwards Sales Process*, your clients will fall into one of these three categories:

1. PROSPECTS: People with whom you are prospecting for new business. These are new customers or customers who have not purchased from you in a year. The goal here is to get to a meeting with the client. You are not selling much as of yet.

2. IN-PROGRESS SALES: People with whom you are currently meeting, who are 'in-progress.' They might have a proposal from you or you are waiting to hear back from them.

3. ACTIVE CLIENTS: These are your active customers that you will retain for a lifetime.

It is important to differentiate and segment these clients into the proper category.

The *Selling Backwards Sales Process* has five very distinct steps.

1. Gaining access/new business development/prospecting
2. Hosting great sales calls
3. Presenting great proposals
4. Excellent follow-up
5. Customer retention

Step One of the *Selling Backwards Sales Process*: Gaining Access/Prospecting

What frequently happens is you're *selling* during the *prospecting* phase and quite honestly; most people simply aren't ready to purchase. Put yourself in your customers' shoes. If you don't know the sales executive, and you don't really know anything at all about them, would you make a decision to buy from them before the first meeting? Not very likely. Impulse buying typically does not happen in the advertising world or the sales world in general. This is why "dialing for dollars" typically does not work. The fact is, a client normally needs to think about a decision before taking action. No sales trick will bypass human nature, which is to stop and evaluate risks. There are exceptions of course, when selling happens without prospecting. For example, when someone is starting a new business or launching a new product and they really have to get on the air or in a publication in a big hurry, they might buy from you during that very first meeting or from your first phone call. That occasional exception is nice of course, but normally, selling during the prospecting phase is off balance – inappropriate even.

So let's be clear. Gaining access means prospecting. Prospecting means getting to a meeting. Nothing more and nothing less. It is very important to make this distinction. You are truly not selling during this phase. Remember, during the prospecting phase, you are trying to get to a meeting with the advertiser! Nothing more. Think about it this way: Since birth, you have been taught not to talk to strangers. Even if you represent a great magazine brand, you are a stranger to the person you are calling on during the prospecting phase. "Stranger danger" is real and it has been engrained in our minds. So, it is highly likely that a new prospect feels uncomfortable doing business with someone they don't know or trust. Why would they buy from you based on one phone call? This is why prospecting is all about getting to a meeting (and not selling) via a phone call or email. You first need to gain their trust.

Here's a hard, cold fact that each and every sales executive should embrace—Advertisers consider most sales executives to be a colossal waste of their time. Sadly, I can't disagree, based on my observations. As I've stated, prospecting is the most difficult phase of the ad sales process. A lot of sales executives suffer from that tired adage, *"You need to work smarter and not harder."* I'm here to tell you that is simply not true. In today's economy, in the digital landscape we're facing currently, you're simply going to have to work a lot harder too. As you'll discover in the next chapter, you're going to learn how to develop a specific, effective prospecting process that includes voice and email templates. You're going to learn about perfect voicemails, e-mailing and follow-up calls until your customers actually respond. Remember, prospecting is the critical first step, regardless of what product you are selling. You need to be working a large group of new clients all the time, or the math is just not going to work in your favor. We will explore these issues in detail in the next chapter.

Step Two of the *Selling Backwards Sales Process*: Hosting Great Sales Calls

Imagine this scenario. After paying a good price for a ticket to the theater, you walk in on opening night, looking forward to an enjoyable evening. The director walks out on stage and says, *"Hello everyone and welcome to our first night. We've never rehearsed this play before, but I think it's going to be great. Sit back, relax and enjoy the show!"* You would be shocked and undoubtedly disappointed. Of course, it might be interesting to watch, but it would be a train wreck!

Believe it or not, this type of scenario happens all the time when sales executives go on sales calls. Like the performers in an unrehearsed play, the sales executives "practice" on their advertisers. They show up at the appointed time, whip out their show-and-tell and start their pitch, oblivious to the disappointment of the audience, (which is their advertiser.) Guess what—rehearsing on a client is a train wreck! Even bigger than this problem, is that the sales executive is oblivious to the failure. Then, they come back to office and blame the client or the economy for the sales failure.

As a professional sales executive, it is important to understand two fundamental parts of human behavior; people dislike change and people don't like taking risks. By nature, the majority of people actually HATE change. Change makes us uncomfortable and people want to avoid feeling uncomfortable. Change represents the unknown, and that's risky. In today's economic environment, advertisers are averse to risk. Period.

When it comes to buying advertising, what are you asking people to do? You're asking them to make a change, make a decision and in some cases, take a risk. You're asking them to make a change and to make a decision about that change – a double negative. I can't stress enough how important it is to understand why advertisers behave the way they do. Is it any wonder that advertisers get put off when you come blowing in for your sales call, armed with all of your tools, Power Points, media kits, talking 100 mph? Add don't forget, the majority of advertisers consider your sales call to be a waste of time. Uphill battle?

Once you accept the fact that your actions during a sales call may disregard your advertiser's normal psychology, you are well on your way to become an improved, more professional sales executive. The fastest way to remove risk, help with change and get an advertiser on your side is to share stories of success. Plus, you will know that you need to stop talking and start educating your advertisers. The way to do that is to ask a lot of critical, meaningful questions during your sales call. Do not ask questions that everyone else asks. Ask great questions with a specific purpose. We will explore these questions and solutions in detail later in the next few chapters.

Step Three of the *Selling Backwards Sales Process*: Presenting Proposals

Most sales people see proposals as the most critical factor of the entire sales process. They truly hang their success on the proposal they send, which is a flawed, yet very common practice. Because we know that the vast majority of people scan and do not read, we are hanging our success on a document that might be 25% read and 75% ignored. Add to that simple fact that most people require visuals to totally comprehend a complex matter and your written proposals are probably helping you lose you a ton of business. I also need to warn you about something. As a sales executive, I rarely send follow-up proposals. Why? Because with my *Selling Backwards Sales Process* I use pricing grids, formulas and data sheets that can be shared on location or over the phone, which saves time and eliminates the need for so many follow-ups to the advertiser.

If you do have to write proposals or if you're creating pricing grids, the thing to remember is this: Keep it simple. Very simple! I like to limit my proposals to two pages or less. If I'm using a pricing grid, I'll limit it to two or three sheets that I'll leave behind with the Marketing Director or business owner. I have become a master at equipping my liaison with the tools they need to get my deal signed. Why not meet with the decision maker? Really? How often does that actually happen? Remember, I sell every day and do not just train and coach.

Many of you develop gorgeous proposals that have been laboriously crafted. Unfortunately, the advertisers often view the proposals as a "book" and will quickly flip through the beautiful pages – ignoring all the details—and go straight to the last few paragraphs where they know they can find the price. As a former decision- maker, I had numerous proposals come across my desk. Every time I picked one up to read, I would read the first paragraph or two (at the most) and then flip to the back of the proposal to find the price. When you create a proposal, consider the reader's perspective. It's not that advertisers are rude people and don't want to read your whole proposal. But they are busy people and have to get things done in a timely manner. We will take a detailed look at this issue as well as pricing grids for success in further chapters of this book.

Step Four of the *Selling Backwards Sales Process*: Excellent Follow Up

I can't tell you the number of times that I have been on the buying-end of a sales call and the sales executive never followed up with me. Or, they follow up four times via email and then gave up. In some cases, I was truly and totally sold and yet nothing was sent to me. Or, I was on vacation or business travel and did not have time or the willingness to respond to the email. The lack of follow-up in the sales industry is astounding! Now, before you doubt me or say that the offending sales executive should be fired, understand that this happens a lot more than you might think.

A few months ago, I was talking to an advertiser that ran in one of the very top consumer magazines in the country. They were sharing an experience they had with a sales executive who came in, made an excellent pitch but never followed up with them. Incredible! I actually knew this sales executive personally, so I called her. She admitted her fault. She had completely forgotten to follow up with her advertiser. And it was a $150,000 deal! Clearly she was mortified, but there was simply no way to recover this sale. In another example, I signed an ad insertion contract and the executive never followed up with me to get the ad. Two months went by and they sent me a bill for an ad that never ran. Then I was given ten excuses and very little solid resolution. This happens all the time. ALL THE TIME!

Moral of that story: Follow up! Period!

Use the wonderful technology that is available. Use a Customer Relationship Management (CRM) program to make reminders for yourself. Put it on your calendar. Put a sticky note on your computer. Write on your hand if you have to, but do something TODAY that will improve your ability to follow up. This is a skill that I can't over emphasize. It's crucial to your success as a sales executive.

The process of following up is twofold. First, creating the perfect pattern for success. Next, understand the client's decision-making process.

We will dig deep on this step later in the book. I will share with you my winning process for follow-up.

Step Five of the *Selling Backwards Sales Process*:
Client Retention

Client retention is the final step in the *Selling Back-wards Sales Process.* What is <u>your</u> client retention plan? Once you've sold an advertiser something, what is your weekly/monthly/annual process that you use to keep that advertiser around for the long term? I ask these questions frequently when I go to a client's location for coaching. Not surprisingly, nine out of ten companies have <u>no</u> plan or process they have developed for client retention. I'll ask them if they're calling their customers, sending out emails, doing a bonus bucks program or any number of actions that can be considered in a good client retention plan. Selling to a new client is far more expensive than retaining a current client. This is an undisputed fact, yet most companies have no customer retention plan beyond Christmas cards. If you know that selling a new client is more expensive, then why on earth do most companies not have a quality retention plan in place? The answer is all over the map. But, nearly all companies have one thing in common when it comes to a lack of a client retention plan... bad excuses. I mean really bad excuses. *Not enough staff. Not enough time. Not enough money.* Excuses abound even in the face of obvious benefits. I'll go into greater detail later in the book and offer dozens of examples of what you can be doing to retain the clients you have.

Ok, so there are the 5 steps to the *Selling Backwards Sales Process*. Now, let me ask you a question. If you had a dozen qualified mechanics in one room with all the parts of an automobile, could they assemble that automobile? Of course they could. But, how many could they assemble in one day? One? Two? The point is there is a reason Henry Ford pioneered the assembly line process. It reduced stress, it was immensely more cost-efficient, and it enabled Ford to track and monitor every individual step involved with manufacturing an automobile. Best of all, it enabled them to discover where the problems were of any given step along the way.

The *Selling Backwards Sales Process* is really the same model. It enables YOU to become measurably more efficient in every single action you take when selling. Plus, it allows you to find repeatable patterns of success. I know you've heard numerous experts say, *"Failure to plan is planning to fail."* I like to say, *"Absence of a sales process equals an absence of significant sales success."* Notice I did not say,

"… An absence of sales" I said *"…an absence of significant sales success."* The emphasis is *"…significant. "* Sales people with no

process can pay their bills and see some success. But my hope is you are reading this book to become a media sales superstar. You want to see significant sales in your future! This is VERY interesting—when writing this book, I looked up the definition of *significant* in the dictionary. This is what I found:

Sig-nif-i-cant, adjective. Sufficiently great or important to be worthy of attention; noteworthy. "a significant increase in sales."

HOLY COW! Even the *Webster's Dictionary* mentions sales! I have coached several thousand sales people in my career. Every single superstar sales executive that I have encountered had one thing in common, a <u>significant</u> and measurable sales process.

So let's dig deep into the *Selling Backwards Sales Process* one step at a time.

CHAPTER THREE

Gaining access, The Big 50 Prospecting Plan

H aving been in the media sales and marketing business since 1996, I can say with authority – I feel your pain! I know what's it like to be an ad sales executive, where each and every day is not always perfect, and where the act of prospecting has to take a back seat to all the other obligatory tasks. But, that's precisely why you must have a disciplined sales process. One part of the sales process I have developed and have taught all over the world is called *"The Big 50 Prospecting Plan,"* and it has been phenomenally successful.

Before we go on, let's make sure that we are clear on several issues. Prospecting is not as much about selling as it is setting appointments to sell. There are three phases of the sales process; prospecting, in-progress sales and retention.

Very often, sales people are trying to sell during the prospecting phase. This is a massive error that I see all of the time. Prospects don't know you, so they certainly are not ready to buy on the spot. There are some products that are sold on the first call; however, in the media business, you will close less than 1% of your sales on the first call. So, each step we walk through in the *Big 50 Prospecting Plan* is all about getting to a meeting where we can use other new skills to close the deal. As I mentioned before, even if you represent a great magazine brand you are a stranger to the person you are calling on during the prospecting phase. "Stranger danger" is real and it has been engrained in our minds since birth. So, it is highly likely that a new prospect feels uncomfortable doing business with someone they don't know and trust. Thus, why would they buy from you based on one phone call? This is why prospecting is all about getting to a meeting not selling via a phone call or email.

I like to compare prospecting with working out. If you work out at the local gym once a week, that's great, and it sure beats zero exercise. But if you were to visit your gym every other day, or a couple of days a week, the results and benefits you would receive from having a regime would be tremendous! As you read through this chapter, think about my analogy of working out, because it really fits my *Big 50 Prospecting Plan* – both require repetition, dedication and discipline to achieve the desired results. And, like many of the processes and methods I teach, I have broken down the processes into smaller steps for clarity and understanding.

The Big 50 Prospecting Plan requires 5 steps for success:

Step 1: Understanding and working "sales math" to your advantage.

Step 2: Defining the perfect prospect.

Step 3: Creating your Big 50 list of prospects.

Step 4: Working these prospects on the perfect pattern for success.

Step 5: Creating great prospecting templates to save you time.

I am often asked for a step-by-step process to sales success. I hope you will see that in this book I will provide details for each step in an effort to improve your chances of success.

Step 1 of the Big 50 Prospecting Plan: Understanding and working math to your advantage.

You need a full funnel to be a raging success in sales. Often in sales training, you'll hear this referred to as "the pipe- line." Whatever you choose to call it, you must constantly be working on new prospects. I can share with you emphatically that every time I've had the most success in my sales career, it was when I had a full hopper of prospects. I think you would agree that sales is as much about having good relationships as it is a numbers game! You need to be working a lot of pros- pects actively if you wish to achieve superstar status with your sales career.

But, how do you do it and get everything else in your day done? I get it. Each day is not a good day in sales land. Your boss sends you 10 emails that require an immediate re- ply. The production department needs this or that. The edito- rial team clearly does not want you to make any money, etc. etc. *(Insert slight laugh here.)* Knowing the "math" behind your sales success is critical. I call this my call-to-close ratios of success. Ask yourself these questions: How many prospecting calls do you need to make before you get a meeting with an advertiser? How many meetings do you have with advertisers before you present a proposal? How many proposals do you present before you close a deal? This is "sales math" at its finest in action. If you were like me, you sat in middle school and asked yourself how all of that math would really help you in life. Well here it is, back to haunt your very sales life.

In nearly every media company with whom I've worked, the answer starts with a list of 50 prospects. I have run these numbers for media companies large and small. The answer keeps coming back to 50. This is why I call this part of the *Selling Backward Sales Process* my *Big 50 Prospecting Plan*. You will need to be working 50 new prospects every 30 days to get 10 meetings. From those 10 meetings you will present 7 proposals. From those 7 proposals you will close 3 deals. This is very standard for most sales people I coach. Obviously, over time, you want to improve those numbers. But just imagine if you could close three brand new deals this month! It all comes back to math and 50 is the number that I work from with nearly every account executive I coach.

Now, keep in mind, you are not starting with 50 and then working down to zero. You should always have 50 on your list. When you book a meeting with someone on your Big 50 list, you move them from "prospect" status to "in-progress" status in your CRM tool. Then, you place a new prospect on your list to replace the one you just removed. Your Big 50 is a living document. You will work each prospect on the Big 50 for 30 days using the methods defined in this chapter. Any person on your Big 50 list that does not respond to you in 30 days comes off the list and is either traded, deleted or marked as inactive in the CRM. Ok, now you need to create your list of 50. So, who are the best prospects to place on the Big 50? Let's move to step #2.

Step 2 of the Big 50 Prospecting Plan: Defining the perfect prospect.

Now that you understand that prospecting is the process of getting a meeting with a new advertiser, I want to help you understand how to define the perfect prospect. As I work with clients, I frequently hear complaints that their sales reps don't seem to be meeting with the right type of prospects. This is a valid concern, because prospecting the wrong advertisers is a huge waste of time, effort and energy. Sales reps that are new to the business are the ones guiltiest of this practice, but I've observed veteran sales executives making the same mistake.

Here are seven qualifications that will help you identify a
good advertising prospect:

1. **They are active in the market.** If your prospect is
currently running TV, radio, newspaper and/or other kind of
ads in various media, then they are active in the market.
They're already spending money on advertising, and this
qualifies them as a good prospect. You won't have to spend
time trying to convince them to go from nothing to something.
Remember, people hate change! The big exception to this rule
is brand new businesses that have never advertised. Also, I am
not looking to make my job harder. Advertisers that are active
in the market normally do not need to be convinced that advertising works.

2. **They show signs of need.** A good advertising prospect will show signs that they need to advertise or market their
product or service. Maybe they offer promotions or specials
on a regular basis. Perhaps they announce new products with
some type of regularity. Perhaps they open up new branches
or offices. A great prospect to have is someone who shows
signs of need on a very regular basis. Discovering their need
for advertising requires some research on your part. Check
their website frequently and check their press releases often.
A really awesome tool is "Google Alerts," which are emails

sent to you when Google finds new results such as newspaper articles, blogs or web pages that match the search terms you've created. Google alerts are as effective as they are easy to use, and will help you monitor your prospects for signs of advertising need.

3. They have a budget. If your prospect is currently active in the market, they typically have some type of budget. What you want to avoid is spending time, effort and energy with an advertiser who has no budget. If they don't have the dollars to spend, the best proposal on the planet won't close a sale. Keep in mind, later in the book we will talk about handling objections when money is the big issue on the advertisers' mind.

4. They have run in the past. You should be looking for prospects that have run advertising in your kind of media in the past. If you're a magazine, have they run in magazines before? If you're in TV, have they done TV commercials before? By the way, I'm never afraid of prospects who didn't have good success with my company's products in the past, because I wasn't there, and don't know all the details of previous campaigns. Remember to ask your prospect about what their experiences were with previous advertising. What ads worked for them? What products did NOT work for them, and why?

Don't be afraid to go back to the prospects that weren't happy about previous campaigns because you just never know what it was that soured the deal.

5. They have a marketing director. You'll hear many top training coaches recommend that you deal only with the top decision-maker while in the midst of your sales process, but realistically, in the advertising world, this very rarely happens. I love dealing with marketing directors. They're more approachable than the company owners, they know their jobs well and, assuming you gain their trust, they're very willing to collaborate with you to get your products sold. That's also why it's so important to provide good proposals that are easy to understand and include good visuals. Educate the marketing director about your products and they will help sell your proposal to their boss. Remember, when prospects have marketing directors, they will usually have marketing budgets! Usually.

6. Look to avoid hard sells. Some of you reading this book might actually enjoy the hard sell, because you love a challenge. That's fine, if that's your thing. However, while you're chasing after that one crazy elusive fish using your methods, you could be catching tons of other pre-qualified fish using my Big 50 process. Over time, the dollars earned from pre-qualified fish will far outweigh the difficult commission earned from that one crazy fish you just had to catch. That's not to say you should NEVER go after the big whales but, typically you will have a higher success rate if you avoid prospects that are a hard sell. I recall hearing a man say to his pal as they sat at a slot machine late one night, *"I am not leaving until I get my money back out of this machine."* Sure, laugh with me on this one right? Will he ever win his money back? Probably one day. Casino experts will tell you that if you play long enough you will hit the big payouts. But do YOU have the time?

Interesting enough, many sales people chase after that elusive hard to close jackpot prospect because of the thrill of the chase. I once heard a slot machine winner say that he spent $2,500 to win $3,000 and it took him *only* 12 hours. Really? Let's try to not be this guy in the sales game.

7. Do quality research on the prospect. Ok, this one is the last piece of the prospect puzzle. What information can you find on *LinkedIN* or *Facebook* that can help you quickly connect with the prospect? There really is no reason to cold call any more because you have some detailed information at your finger tips. Let me give you an example: A prospect of mine, Carol Deeds, was about to be placed on my Big 50 list. I looked on *LinkedIN* to find out if there were any connection points we might share. One interesting thing jumped off the page at me. We both shared a common passion for boating. I made a note of this as well as some other information such as her past employers, where she attended college, etc. in my Customer Relations Management (CRM) tool. Armed with this information, I began to work my Big 50 list, as shown in the next few paragraphs, and I wove into my process the personal information I had found online. Keep in mind, knowing the difference between creepy and relevant information is the key to creating a connection without coming across as weird. I have found that using this method increases my chances of connection with the client by over 50%! I think we all know that there is a ton of information about us and others online, so before I mention information to a prospect, I identify where I found it. For example, *"Carol, I saw on LinkedIN that we share a common passion for boating."*. I recommend that you don't mention kids, boyfriends, martial status or anything like that because that might be a little personal to the prospect, even if they have posted about it on social media. I have NEVER, EVER had a person feel uncomfortable with me over this approach. As a sales professional, you may not be comfortable with this "shared information" approach because you are stuck on 1990 when cold calling was how you learned about people. Wake up. The 90's are calling and they want you back. People share their information online for a reason. Use it!

As you're preparing your Big 50 prospect list, keep in mind the seven qualifications of a good prospect detailed here. Print this list and put it by your computer. Don't add a prospect to your prospecting list unless they meet at least three of the qualifications. Don't put anybody on your list if you know absolutely nothing about them. If you want to have outstanding sales success, you need to define your perfect sales prospect so that you are truly prospecting the right people.

Step 3 of the Big 50 Prospecting Plan: Creating your Big 50 list of prospects.

Once you fully understand what makes a good prospect, you're ready to create your "Big 50 Prospect List." Use Excel, Word, Google Docs or whatever works best for you to create your list. Then, you can make adjustments to the accounts in your CRM tool.

First create 5 columns across the top of the page using the days of the week. One column for each day of the work week. Under each column header, you list 10 new prospect names, for a total for 50 new prospect names. Note, five columns, five days and 10 prospects under each day of the week. Now, what qualifies a prospect as "new"? I would say that new is someone that has not run or bought from you in the last 6 months. There are always circumstances that mess up the 6-month criteria. So, be careful not to over complicate this process. If you have an advertiser that needs to be renewed, you can place them on this list too. Many sales reps keep clients on their prospect lists for years. This is a bad business practice. Hoping that someone will close "eventually" is not smart. I will often write down the 50 prospects before I enter the prospects into my customer relations management (CRM) tool.

Besides the days of the week, you may also want to categorize each day by industry or a local category. For example, your 10 names for Monday might all be lawyers. This allows your brain to stay on a focused conversation while you are prospecting that day. (This is not required but many sales people find this to be helpful.) Please note that once I am happy with my list and it has been approved by my boss, I add all my Big 50 into my CRM tool or I login to the CRM tool and tag the correct prospects with "Big 50", so I can manage them. Remember, if the prospect does not meet at least three of my criteria for being a good prospect than I DO NOT add them to my list. The creation of a quality list is critical. As you are adding them to your CRM tool, do not forget to add in the notes on the CRM—the business research plus any non-creepy personal information you know about them to make them a great prospect.

Ok, let's get them added to your CRM. Each CRM will handle this differently. Let me give you an example. Many of my magazine customers use The Magazine Manager® as their CRM and production process tool. In The Magazine Manager® you can create categories for each client. For example, lawyers, doctors, banks. But, you can also create a priority. If you are using my Big 50 plan, your priorities would be prospects, in-progress and active. Along with numerous other relevant features, this makes The Magazine Manager® my choice of CRM for the magazine ad sales industry. One of the issues I often see is that each and every client in the CRM is marked as "active". This will hurt your sales process because you are not able to pull and manage your Big 50 list each and every day with ease. Remember, one of the things I want to do is save you time and reduce your stress. So, this type of customization is critical. Now let's say you are using a simple CRM tool like Highrise® from software company 37 Signals. You can create "tags" for each client like "big 50" or "Ryan's list". This allows you to search lists within your CRM for sending mass emails and is also a way to better organize your accounts. Better organization is critical to your success. Nearly every successful sales rep I know uses a CRM tool. Each of these super-star ad sales reps lives and dies by their CRM tool. One of the secrets to Big 50 success is going to be in the patterns you use to connect with your prospects. Without a CRM it will be almost impossible to keep up with the high level of activity that I am about to coach you through toward sales success.

Step 4 of the Big 50 Prospecting Plan: Working these prospects on the perfect pattern for success

Remember my example about working out in the gym? Prospecting is similar in that if you only prospect a client once or twice a month, your results are going to be marginal. You will be very 'forgettable' in the minds of your prospect. If you add the fact that most sales people only email and do not pick up the phone at all, you have a double whammy of bad luck. To illustrate my point, let's use John from Hillsdale Services as my sample prospect on my Big 50 list. Suppose you contact John from Hillsdale on a Monday and leave a voice mail. If John had a bad day for whatever reason, what is the likelihood of him even remembering your voicemail? What are the chances of him returning your call? Pretty low! You are very forgettable! That's why I like to create a "pattern of persistence" when contacting my advertisers. I strive to be politely persistent, versus annoyingly persistent, a subtle difference that your advertisers will appreciate. I use a combination of voice mail and email touches to get to a meeting with the client. I also use numbered templates to keep my message focused, consistent and to be sure that I do not say the same thing twice in a row. We will dig into these templates in the next and last step of the prospecting plan.

Here's how the *Big 50 Prospecting Plan* works: I will call AND email John every third business day for thirty days. Yes, I said every 3rd business day for 30 days! Now, some of you may be thinking, *"Whoa Ryan! There's no possible way I'm going to contact somebody that often!"* Before you throw the book down, let me ask you a question: Have you ever forgotten to return a phone call or reply to an email from a friend? Ok, we all have. That is a person that you knew and liked. So, just imagine the psychology behind what I am teaching. Because 99% of the prospects you're calling don't even know you, your first attempts to contact them will have marginal results. People don't like talking to strangers. Plus, people are very busy; 75% of those you contact will be too busy to return the call. What a losing battle right? No, because we are never going to place someone on our Big 50 list without some type of personal research to help us cut through the "stranger danger" issue. If you just drop one name, a hobby or past connection, your chances of sparking their interest grows exponentially. Share a quick success story or a competitors name and you will increase your chances of getting through greatly. Don't worry; I will share my prospecting templates with you in a minute. The problem I see is generic sales people that leave generic voice mails or generic emails and they do this once per month and then blame the client for not replying. What? This is the prospects' fault?

Ok, here is my formula for success in this phase of the prospecting process:

1. **Use voice mail templates.** Call the prospect and leave a VERY relevant voice mail that contains a new idea, success story and/or a small tidbit of personal data to perk their interest.

2. **Then immediately email the prospect.** After you leave the voice mail, email the prospect a VERY relevant new idea, success story and/or a small tidbit of personal data to perk their interest. Three sentences max.

3. **Repeat this pattern with a new template every third business day for 30 days.** Each contact is a new idea, issue, etc. Never leave the same voice mail or send the same email. The idea is to vary your messages in an effort to peak their interest.

4. **They will eventually return your message in some way.** You will probably get an email. When they do contact you, move them to a meeting and also to the "in-progress" status in your CRM. Then replace them on the Big 50 list with a new prospect.

I can't tell you the number of times I have worked this plan for 2 weeks and then get a reply. People have either returned my calls or left a voice mail and said, "*Ryan, thank you for your voice mails – it reminded me that I needed to get back* with you." Or, "*Oh yeah Ryan, sorry man I have been so busy. Thanks for checking back with me.* " People are busy and simply don't have the time to do all the things required in a business day.

If you are still thinking "there is no possible way" that you willing or able to contact your prospect every third business day, let me provide an example. "Dave" was a marginally-performing sales person that worked for a very large publishing company. Dave was a really great guy, but he simply wasn't very persistent in his prospecting. He had no long-term success, and his prospecting numbers were very low. Dave was one of those guys who sat in the back of one of my workshops with an attitude of "*Nah, I really don't believe in this, I know I'm going to get negative feedback if I use the Big 50 plan of attack.*" So I gave Dave a challenge. I told him to try contacting his prospects on an every-third-day-basis for thirty days; at the end of the thirty days, if his numbers had not improved, I would buy Dave and his wife a steak dinner at the restaurant of their choice. Dave readily accepted my challenge; for thirty days, he contacted his prospects every 3rd business day without fail using my Big 50 pattern and a version of my templates. At the end of the thirty days, Dave had more meetings with advertisers than he had ever had in his entire sales career! Quite honestly, Dave wasn't that great of a sales rep. But using the Big 50 method, he had a pattern that he could replicate and then repeat. He had found a pattern of repeatable success. Dave is proof that the system works – it creates a pattern, it creates consistency and it reduces randomness. It really works!

Now, last step. What do you say via email? What do you say when you leave a voice mail? Before we jump into templates, I am often asked about the optimum time of day to prospect? The answer is normally 11:30am and 4:30pm. Why? Most people do not book meetings at 11:30am for fear that the meeting will interrupt their lunch. And, most people do not book meetings at 4:30pm for fear that the meeting will interrupt their ability to leave at 5pm. Keep in mind; every market and industry is different. So, test and re-test until you find the perfect time. All in all, randomness kills your process. DO NOT be random. Do things with a purpose. Do things with a passion. I have never met a successful person that lived every day by random occurrences of greatness. You make greatness each and every day of your life. You control your destiny. You control the level of success you wish to achieve. Life is about the choices you make. Sure, some people have better options, but the best stories of success are about those people that make great choices when given almost nothing in life. Sales success is no different.

Step 5 of the *Big 50 Prospecting Plan*: Creating great prospecting templates to save you time and increase your chances of success.

Templates are critical to saving you time, effort and energy. When you create your templates, there are 4 important factors to consider for "voice mail and email success:

1. **Make sure to be very relevant.** You want to include the client's name or product name. Be very specific. *"Hi John, I see your promoting your ABC 300 Model."*

2. **Be sure to mention a quick story of success.** *"Your competitor, Rex Reed has been marketing with us and reported solid success."* Or mention a new idea. *"I have a new idea for you that could increase your sales."*

3. **Promise not to waste his time.** *"John, I pride myself in not wasting people's time. I truly feel this is a great idea for you."*

4. **Keep it short.** Remember, prospects are looking to delete your voice mail or email. They are not looking to read or listen. So, be brief and relevant.

Ok, with these four factors in mind, we will create 6 to 10 templates that we will use each time we contact John. I will share several with you now. Let's go back and think about how to handle John on our Big 50 list. On Monday at 11:30am, contact John via phone, and leave your voice message using template #1. Immediately after leaving the voice mail you will send an email that contains the same information. You will then log in to your CRM and set a reminder to contact him in 72 hours. *"Hi, John. I see your promoting your ABC 300 Model on TV. Your competitor, Rex Reed has been marketing with me this month and reported solid success. John, I pride myself in not wasting people's time. I truly feel this is a great idea for you. I'll drop you an email about this idea as well. This is Ryan from Bluewater News. 803-867-5309."* Notice that I did not say my name or company name first. NEVER, ever do this. I know, call me crazy. You have probably been doing this for years. Stop. This is a sure fire way to get deleted.

Ok, 72 hours later. Maybe try him at 4:30pm this time. Let's roll out with template #2. Remember, you need to consider the 4 factors as noted about voice mail and email success when you create your own templates. Remember, voice mail followed by an immediate email. *"Hi John. I'd like to share a way we can put the Model ABC 300 in front of 35,000 new customers in the next 30 days. I just sent you an email too. I promise not to waste your time. This is Ryan from Bluewater News. 803-867-5309."* Ok, good job. Now log this in your CRM and set your next reminder for 72 hours later.

Another 72 hours pass. Maybe try him at 11:30am this time. Let's roll out template #3. Remember, you need to consider the 4 factors as noted about voice mail and email success when you create your own templates. Remember, voice mail and then an immediate email. In this template I am going to mention 2 of his competitors by name. *"Hi John. Dynmax and Reliant are both seeing solid success with us these days. I truly feel that I have something new and creative to offer. I just sent you an email too. I promise not to waste your time John. I hate sales people that waste my time. This is Ryan from Bluewater News. 803-867-5309."*

Notice that each voice mail and email message is slightly different from the one left previously. Why? There's no reason to repeat the exact message in each progressive voice mail/email that you send, since the contact did not provide the expected response. This method is an ice-breaking technique. You are trying to crack the nut and get a response from an advertiser.

My goal is to create templates that make this process easy to execute. I can contact 10-30 prospects per day with ease. This pattern tells the prospect that you are serious and you are not giving up. Also, by using different voice message templates and different email templates, you're being politely persistent in achieving your goal, which is to get a response. There are only two sides to a response. "Go" or "No. " A 'go' might be, *"Yeah, give me more information about your offer/product."* A 'no' might be , *"I'm the wrong person, you need to contact someone else in our company."* And sometimes a 'no' is simply that – *"NO, we're not interested."*

What defines a great voice mail and email message? First and most importantly, your messages should be short, short, short! You would not believe some of the emails I receive from ad sales reps, messages that are paragraphs long, and seemingly endless! I actually cringe when I open one of those emails. So do your advertisers!

Another point to consider when sending a business email is the subject line. You already know that business people today get hundreds of emails weekly. Are you aware that over half of emails are now read via a smart phone? Your subject line must be specific and attention getting. The first sentence of the email should encourage the recipient to open the email, rather than hit the delete button. The last thing you want is to be deleted, so consider your subject line carefully.

Here are several that work for me:

1. For your consideration
2. A quick note for you
3. Quick chat with you?
4. Five minutes for a new idea?
5. "_____" is really doing well. (Insert competitor's name)

The emails and voice mail templates should never be about YOU. You will need to create your own templates and test them out on your own. Should you expect your prospect to always answer your voice mails? I don't. But I'm different from a lot of sales coaches in that I actually LIKE leaving voice mails, and recommend you do the same. Why? Because leaving high quality, frequent voice messages helps you become a known entity; remember, humans don't like doing business with people they don't know! And, contacting your prospect with high frequency helps you advance your marketing message.

I still sell to this day. So as a sales executive, my prospects phone me back approximately half the time, which is better than average. What I see most often is my prospects reply via email. Let's face it. Today, email is the preferred method of communication for most business people for a lot of different reasons. It stands to reason the better you communicate with email, the higher likelihood of success. Now, if I can get a meeting face to face – Boy! - I can really knock it out of the park, and you may be the same way. However, that doesn't happen very often anymore; if you have national accounts, it rarely happens.

I think you would agree that in the markets that any of us serve, whether it be in television, radio, newspaper or magazine sales, the advertisers are inundated with phone calls and emails from sales reps. Even in the smaller markets, there are 15-20 mainstream media outlets from which advertisers can choose. In the New York area, there are over 200! Los Angeles – over 200, Boston - over 125. Advertisers have more choices than they have time to choose, relative to their marketing dollars. What are you going to do to stand out from the crowd? How can you make sure your message is heard above all the others?

One of the things you can control is repetition-- by having high repetition and quality voice mails and emails. You are not going to leave the same 'ole voice mail everyone else does, like *"Hi Bob, it's Ryan Dohrn calling from ABC Magazine...got a great issue on such and such coming up...would love to chat about it."* So, how can you leave a voice message that will help the prospect remember you? First of all, you're not going to leave your name, rank and serial number. That's a sure fire way to have your voice mail deleted. Mentioning your prospect's name and their company name and/or products will help prevent your message from getting deleted – people love to hear the sound of their own name and their company name. I will give you exact voice mail templates later in the book.

Once you are happy with your voice message and email templates, you're ready to work your Big 50 list using the pattern described in the previous step. I hope you don't use my templates and start making calls like a telemarketer because that's not my intention! For one thing, the templates I've suggested may not work specifically for YOUR prospects – you really should spend some time to customize your own templates. Use your own communication style and tone.

Ok, let's wrap up this chapter. Remember there are five steps to the *Big 50 Prospecting Plan.*

Step 1: Understanding and working "sales math" to your advantage.

Step 2: Defining the perfect prospect.

Step 3: Creating your Big 50 list of prospects.

Step 4: Working these prospects on the perfect pattern for success.

Step 5: Creating great prospecting templates to save you time.

Again, just in case you missed this point, we are going to repeat this pattern with a new template every third business day for 30 days. Each contact is a new idea, issue, etc. We will never leave the same voice mail or send the same email. The idea is to vary our message in an effort to peak their interest. Your Big 50 is a living document. You will work each prospect on the Big 50 for 30 days using the methods defined in this chapter. Any person on your Big 50 list that does not respond to you in 30 days comes off the list and is either traded, deleted or marked as inactive in the CRM.

If a prospect becomes inactive on your list, consider trading some accounts with a peer sales rep. Some of you are VERY averse to trading accounts, I know. Why would you trade your prospects with another sales rep, especially after all of your hard work? You know what's going to happen, right? Your peer sales rep will make one call, and the prospect is going to call him or her back! But, if you all trade prospects, the likelihood of the same thing happening to you is very high. Either way, it's wise to give your non-responding prospects a break for 30 days, and then go back to them and try again.

You may be wondering how much time will be required to work your Big 50 list. Once you've developed your pattern, you'll find that it requires approximately 30 minutes in the morning and 30 minutes in the afternoon. If you follow my pattern of every 3 days correctly, you will have many days with 10 and 10. If you think you don't have time to work your list religiously, daily and without fail, you need to MAKE the time!

Prospecting is absolutely fundamental to sales success. Most people don't do it often enough, they don't have a pattern and they don't use a process. I've said it a hundred times, but you need to work harder, AND be smarter about it.

Final note: As you work your list you may have a prospect every now and again that will say something like, *"Hey Ryan, you are really annoying, calling me all the time."* But just because you get one person who doesn't appreciate your tenacity and persistence, don't stop moving forward! Don't stop doing what you need to do in order to be a raging success. I wouldn't insist on you using my process if I didn't know how successful it will be for you. I've experienced the success and I've had my coaching clients share their success stories with me. Remember, if ad sales were easy, everybody would be doing it!

Ok, so now you are a prospecting master. You should be getting more meetings. So, what do you do to maximize the success of these meetings? Let's move on to the next step in the *Selling Backwards Sales Process*.

Here are more templates you might consider reformatting for your sales needs:

#1: *"Hi _____, I'd like to share a way we can put*

_____ in front of 35,000 new customers in the next 30

days. I just sent you a voicemail/email too. I promise not to

waste your time. I pride myself in being a sales person that will

only bring you ideas that matter to your business! This is Ryan

from Chicago Living at 888-812- 9991. Again, it's Ryan at 888-

812-9991. Thank you _____. " (Say your phone num-

ber slowly.)

#2. *"Hi _____, I have a new idea for _____ that*

is really working for some of my other clients. I just sent you an

email about it as well. I would love to chat about it with you for

just a quick second. Again, I promise not to waste your time. I

pride myself in being a sales person that will only bring you

ideas that matter to your business! This is Ryan from Chicago

Living at 888-812-9991. Again, it's Ryan at 888-812-9991.

*Thank you for your time." (*Say your phone number slowly.)

#3: *"Hi _____. I'm calling for some product and marketing*

information on _____. I'll email you too. This is Ryan

from Chicago Living at 888-812-9991. Again, it's Ryan at 888-

812-9991. Thank you for your time." (Say your phone number

slowly.)

#4: *"Hi _____. I'm calling because I have a perfect marketing fit for _____ in the upcoming edition of Chicago Living. I've emailed you about it as well. I promise not to waste your time. I hate it when people waste my time! This is Ryan from Chicago Living at 888-812-9991. Again, it's Ryan at 888-812-9991. Thank you for your time."* (Say your phone number slowly.)

#5: *"Hi _____. Mark, over at (-----Insert competitor----,) is having some great success as our marketing partner. I truly think this is worth your time. I promise to not waste your time. Five minutes is all I need. I sent an email to you as well. This is Ryan from Chicago Living at 888-812-9991. Again, it's Ryan at 888-812-9991. Thank you for your time."* (Say your phone number slowly.)

#6: *"Hi _____. Just in case I'm leaving messages for the wrong person … I wanted to confirm that you are the marketing contact/person at _____? If there is someone else I should get in touch with, please let me know. I'll email this question to you, too. This is Ryan from Chicago Living at 888-812-9991. Again, it's Ryan at 888-812-9991. Thank you for your time."* (Say your phone number slowly.)

#7: *"Hi _____. I wanted to see if you had any upcoming events or upcoming specials you are having at _____ that we may be able to help promote. Maybe we could do a partnership together? I'll email you. This is Ryan from Chicago Living at 888-812-9991. Again, it's Ryan at 888-812-9991. Thank you for your time."* (Say your phone number slowly.)

#8: *"Hi _____. Good news, I'm not selling insurance or calling from the IRS! Part of my job is to help you market your business. You can probably tell from the number of times I have called you that I am serious about my job. I have been selling in this market for 10 years. I can help you _____. I'm sure you know who this is, it's Ryan from Chicago Living at 888-812-9991. Again, it's Ryan at 888- 812-9991. Thank you for your time."* (Say your phone number slowly.)

#9: *"Hi _____. I saw your ad in _____. It looked great! Wanted to talk to you about who you want to reach with your marketing messages. I promise not to waste your time. I pride myself in being a sales person that will only bring you ideas that work! Maybe we can help. I'll send you an email about this too. This is Ryan from Chicago Living at 888-812-9991. Again, it's Ryan at 888-812-9991. Thank you for your time."* (Say your phone number slowly.)

#10: *"Hi _____ . I drive by your billboard every day on _____ , and it makes me want to learn more about your business. Could we get together or talk for ten minutes, tops? I'll send you an email about this too. This is Ryan from Chicago Living at 888-812-9991. Again, it's Ryan at 888-812-9991. Thank you for your time."* (Say your phone number slowly.)

#11: *"Hi _____ . I know you advertised with Chicago Living years ago. I'd love to share with you some new things that have happened with the magazine that may help _____ . I'll send you an email about this too. This is Ryan from Chicago Living at 888-812-9991. Again, it's Ryan at 888-812- 9991. Thank you for your time."* (Say your phone number slowly.)

#12: *"Hi _____ . Was just checking out your website, I wanted to ask if you were trying to get more customers to visit your site? I'm not sure if that is important to your business. If it is, I may be able to help _____ . I can email you too. This is Ryan from Chicago Living at 888-812-9991. Again, it's Ryan at 888-812-9991. Thank you for your time."* (Say your phone number slowly.)

Please remember that your templates need to be in a sequential order to avoid repeating or randomness. Many get more aggressive as time goes on.

CHAPTER FOUR

Hosting Great Sales Calls

Your company might have the most innovative, cost-effective marketing solutions available on the market, but if you're not able to host great sales calls, you will never achieve your maximum potential. Everything I teach in this chapter applies to phone and in-person sales. I will be sure to note the subtle differences where they occur.

Many sales executives, who have operated by the seat of their pants for years, struggle in this new digital advertising sales environment. There is no reason to ever go on a sales call and "fly by the seat of your pants" Or, "just wing it". I have worked with countless sales executives on their sales meeting process and the changes I have observed have been dramatic. Those that have a sales call process close far more sales than the very best reps that just "wing it." Having a prepared plan of attack when you begin a sales call is critical to your success.

I have found that there are seven important phases in every sales call. It does not matter if you are in person or on the phone. They are still the same. If you master these phases you will see an increase in sales. Here is an overview of the seven phases and then we will explore them in detail. Once you practice this flow to your sales call enough, it will become second nature. Think of it as a road map on how you can handle each sales call.

7 Important Phases In Every Sales Call:

1. Understanding what roadblocks are right in front of you from the first moment you open your mouth.
2. Opening your meeting with relevant information about the client or company.
3. Sharing success stories to reduce risk.
4. Asking really great questions to better understand your clients needs, goals and desires.
5. Offering your products or solutions only after you understand their needs, goals and desires.
6. Offering an on-site proposal by using visually rich one-sheets and pricing grids.

7. Setting a time for next steps.

Phase #1 of the sales meeting: Understanding what road-blocks are right in front of you from the first moment you open your mouth.

Many rookie ad sales executives think the sales call is all about presenting his/her product, but this isn't necessarily true. In fact, initially, the product you're presenting isn't all that important—instead, your prospect will be busy sizing you up, determining if you're worthy of their time. Advertisers have their own evaluation process to help them make decisions relative to media buys. As an individual, you are under the microscope from the first moment you make your first prospecting call. Now, for the next level.

As I was developing my *Selling Backwards Sales Process*, I did tons of research and picked the brains of several hundred successful marketing directors in small, medium and large companies. I also spoke to many media buyers that work in some of the biggest ad agencies in the world. I asked them to name the top five factors they considered when making the decision whether or not to buy media from an ad sales person.

Their answers, both enlightening and surprising, were used to develop what I call the "sales consideration funnel." These are the questions and concerns that the advertiser thinks about prior to you even opening your mouth. When you understand these factors, then you can better address the advertisers needs during the sales call.

The five factors of the sales consideration funnel are:

1. What will this ad do for me?
2. What will this ad sales person do for me?
3. What will I feature in my ad?
4. Will this ad make me look good to my community and/or my boss?
5. What do I think of the idea and/or the price?

Let's explore each of these five factors so that you can get your head around them and weave these concerns into your sales meeting and sales presentation.

Sales Consideration Factor #1: What will this ad do for me?

The number one consideration when buying media from an ad sales executive is all about return on investment (ROI). The advertiser wants to know what the ad will do for them. How might the ad impact their business? Most importantly, how will your product or solution make them money?

To answer this question (unspoken or not) you need to have a success story to present. The fastest way to remove risk in a buyer's mind is for you to share success stories and ease their concern.

Sales Consideration Factor #2: What will this sales person do for me?

The second consideration in the mind of your advertiser is all about you. Business owners and marketing directors want to know if they can rely on you as their sales rep. Or, are you just like all the rest... a waste of their time; a time- sucking vampire of sales. Then, will you be there for them after the sale? Are you going to help them with their creative? Are you going to follow up with them, or will you just give lip service?

Again, one of the best ways for you to build rapport and minimize risk is to share success stories about you and your business relationships with other clients. Telling your new advertiser you've been an ad sales executive for 12 years is not a success story. However, talking about customers with whom you've built great relationships and friendships with for a lifetime is a good example of a solid success story. Remember advertisers don't buy products from companies, they buy from

YOU. They want and need an ad sales executive in which they can trust, so your job is to convince them.

Sales Consideration Factor #3: What will I feature in my ad?

Advertisers' third consideration deals with the creative process. What are they going to feature in their ads? Who is going to build the ad? What will the ad look like when completed? These concerns are huge roadblocks in the minds of the advertiser, so what are you going to do to overcome these objections?

Not long ago, I was chatting with an ad sales executive about the role of sales people as it relates to the advertisers' creative process. He said he just didn't have the time to *"....hold his customer's hands."* I thought to myself, *"Seriously?"* Walking your customer through the creative process is a fundamental part of being an effective ad sales rep. If you're in the magazine business, bring in a spec ad to share with your advertiser. Cut out ads from national magazines to show them the potential. Create what I call an "ad binder of success." If you're in TV, show them some of the best ads you have to offer on your iPad or Smartphone. The more creative assistance you can offer to your advertiser, the more likely he/she will say yes to your proposal. Remember you're always trying to create the path of least resistance; you're always trying to make it easy for them to say yes!

Sales Consideration Factor #4: Will this ad make me look good to my community and/or my boss?

The fourth concern advertisers consider may surprise you. (It did me!) They want to know if your ad is going to make their company look good to their industry (or community) and/or will it make them look good to their boss? For many marketing directors, the fear of failure is very real. They have to ask for money to authorize an ad campaign. What if the ad does not generate results for the boss or business? They put faith in you that the ad will work. What if it does not? They can blame you all day long, but in the end, they made the recommendation and got the money approved. So, as their ad sales rep, it becomes your job to help them understand the power and effectiveness of advertising. I tell them they need to advertise in "multiple ways on multiple days". Again, sharing success stories about your clients who advertise heavily (and who get great results) is a very effective way of overcoming this concern. In the end, I like to under-promise and over-deliver.

Sales Consideration Factor #5: What do they think of the idea and/price?

The final consideration in my "sales consideration funnel" is a no-brainer. Advertisers consider whether they like the product/idea you've presented, and whether they are agreeable to the price of the product. Remember, price becomes the deciding factor when two products seem similar. So, you will need to create distinct differences between you and your competitor.

As we discuss each phase of the sales call, these five factors and roadblocks will need to be addressed. The most common way to address these issues is by sharing a success story. The important piece of these 5 factors is to recognize that there are predetermined questions and issues rolling around inside the advertisers mind before you even open your mouth. Now that you know these factors, you can address them as you move through the next phase of the sales call.

Phase #2 of the sales meeting: Opening your meeting with relevant information about the client or company. One of your goals as a sales person is to be exceedingly relevant. It is critical to never, ever come across as a generic sales person.

It is important to understand that the time you have to connect with the client comes and goes very quickly. I mentioned before the issues you face with "stranger danger". Since birth people have been told not to talk to strangers. I see it at networking events all the time. In walks a sales person to the party, immediately seeking out people they already know. Why? Because we crave comfort and we reject risk. New people equals risk. LinkedIn has been the best tool for me to beat the "stranger danger" game. I will always refer to the fact that I found out this or that on LinkedIn when talking with someone. I look at each person's profile in detail to find points of connection. I will be sure to add this data to my CRM tool. I will visit their company web site to find out more information and about the company as well. I am looking for any connection points that I can find. You have a very limited window of time to create a connection. No connection, no sale. People buy from people they know and trust. Period. If you are not using LinkedIn, get some training. I offer a LinkedIn webinar on a regular basis. Check it out.

Recently I was preparing to make a sales call. I noticed on LinkedIn that the advertiser on whom I was calling had attended the University of Alabama. In the South, the Southeastern Conference (SEC) reigns supreme in college sports. I am a big fan of the University of South Carolina. This was going to be my connection point on the call. It worked very well. The same day I had a call with a man from New York City. I noticed that he once worked in Chicago like I had. We had an immediate connection. These connection points are critical to starting off a sales call very strong. Also, it proves that you have done your homework! That is very impressive. If you cannot find any shared connections, then go with company connections by referencing products or news items that you found on their company website. I avoid using Facebook to learn about my sales prospects because most of the information on Facebook might seem too personal when mentioned.

Phase #3 of the sales meeting: Sharing success stories to reduce risk.

Human aversion to change and decision-making is well documented, and in Chapter Two, I discussed the rationale behind these human behaviors. The smart ad sales executive understands and accepts these behavioral traits, and uses a proven, time-honored technique to address all five factors in the sales consideration funnel. That technique—share success stories. It is important that all success stories apply directly to the advertiser. This is more difficult than it sounds, apparently. I was recently coaching a client in a meeting with ten ad sales executives. During our meeting, I asked each of them to share a success story with the group. Dead silence. You would have thought I asked them to give blood on the spot, or cut their fingers off, that's how difficult it was for them!

I can't stress this enough. If you want to be really successful in advertising sales, you MUST develop a collection of relevant, factual success stories that can be shared with your advertisers. It's the fastest, most effective way to remove risk, remove doubt and increase the likelihood your advertiser will say yes to your proposal. Success stories help you to paint a "picture of potential" that your advertiser can understand, endorse and feel comfortable with on the spot. No one wants to be the pioneer of the market. By nature, most people are followers. They follow the tribe. There are exceptions to every rule of course. By sharing success stories, you make it easier for the advertiser to make a decision.

As you think about the five factors that advertisers are considering before they buy an ad from you, it is important to have a success story to match each issue. It is important that success stories are the first thing you share on a sales call. If you go directly to your pitch you are dead! DEAD! So, how do you transition to a natural progression of telling these stories and how do you weave in the five factors of consideration too? I like to simply ask this question… *"Do you mind if I share with you the success other business owners like you are having by partnering with us?"* If the client says no, then you truly know where you are at with this client. If a client wants me to cut to the chase, then I proceed and share success stories during the rest of conversation with them. I try to stick to my road map for the sales call and try not to be derailed. I want to prime the sales sequence. We are following a map to success and priming the sequence means I start mentioning the success stories early as a way to prime the buyers mind. What exactly is priming? It is easy to explain.

Scientists refer to priming when they talk about human behavior as it relates to the powers of persuasion. If I tell you to not think of green trees, what do you immediately think about? I have primed you to think of green trees. I have practiced and observed priming in sales and marketing for years. If I can share enough success stories with a buyer, the likelihood that they will give me consideration grows ten fold compared to just pitching an idea without any priming.

For example, let me show you each factor of consideration and I'll share a sample success story that shows how I prime the buyer to consider the idea.

The five factors of the sales consideration funnel are:

1. What will this ad do for me? Sample success story: I shared with a prospect that recently, a client of mine ran an ad for his new product. Because he knew print ads drive web traffic, he hoped the ad would push 200 people to his website. It actually pushed over 700 to the site through a unique website domain name.

2. What will this ad sales person do for me? Sample success story: I pride myself in taking care of my clients. I shared that the owner of RC Limited often refers to me as his right hand marketing man. I have had some marketing clients renew with me every year for over 7 years.

3. What will I feature in my ad? Sample success story: I make sure to point out that we have a dedicated team of graphic designers that will walk you through every-phase of the ad design process. I will even help you pick the pictures and write the ad copy. I personally work with the owner of Mavericks Furniture each month on their ad.

4. Will this ad make me look good to my industry, community or, my boss? Sample success story: I was at a chamber reception last week and Rob Green of Green's Ford told me that his marketing director is amazing, as people at his church tell him every week how much they like seeing his ads on TV.

5. What do I think of the idea and/or the price? Sample success story: Gretchen Smith from Smith's Unlimited told me last week that this idea generated more leads for them in one month than nearly everything they did last year.

I can share three to five success stories in less than 90 seconds. Of course you need to practice. Most sales people need at least ten relevant success stories. If you are talking to a plumber about an ad then you need some service industry success stories. If you are taking to a lawyer, you need some professional services success stories. Don't have any? Get going. Meet as a group. Share success stories at every sales meeting. Ask your clients in person **not via email**. You are not looking to create a sheet of testimonials. You are looking to share true stories of success verbally with your clients.

Phase #4 of the sales meeting: Asking Critical Questions:

After you have success stories out on the table, now it is time to find out how you can help the client. Asking questions helps to manage customer expectations and illustrates to your advertisers that you are interested in their requirements and needs. Asking questions and focusing on what the advertiser needs is infinitely more acceptable than you talking endlessly about your products and offerings. Best of all, asking questions during your sales call helps to lead the conversation to where YOU want it to go. It is important to note that I am not asking questions to get a conversation going. I am asking questions with a purpose. If I ask good questions I can then tailor my pitch or presentation to the clients' exact needs. This allows me to make the presentation personalized and not generic. I often use the analogy that making sales calls is a lot like playing a game of chess. A good chess player is always thinking several moves ahead. The great chess player knows every move they're going to make all the way through the end of the match. They are able to anticipate what their opponent is going to do, and are ready to respond with the move they had planned. This is exactly how you should play your sales game.

I am not looking to ask a broad question like *"Tell me about your marketing plans for this year."* Or, *"Tell me a little bit more about your business."* These are typical ad sales questions that make advertisers groan. I want to ask better questions. I want to ask the questions that other media sales executives are <u>NOT</u> asking. The questions you develop for your sales calls aren't just conversation-starters. Like the chess player who is thinking ahead, you should have a goal or an objective in mind. I like to call the best of the questions my *10 Critical Questions*.

Here are my top **10 Critical Sales Questions** to ask your advertisers during a sales call:

Question #1: *"If we could create the perfect ad for you, what would it look like and what would you want to happen from that ad?"* Your objective behind this question is very specific. It helps you to manage your advertiser's expectations. Their response will help you understand the content of their ad and the creative that will be involved. This question will get them to talk about the results they are expecting from their ad.

Consider this scenario. You are in a sales meeting with your prospect and you ask the question in the previous paragraph. Their response is *"I want this ad to increase my website traffic by 80%."* Yikes! Clearly, this advertiser needs a better understanding of what drives traffic to websites, but see how your question opened the dialogue? Now you can realistically manage your customer's expectations.

Question #2: *"How many times do you feel a new customer of yours needs to see your advertising message before they make a decision to do business with you?"*

If your advertiser responds, *"One,"* then you need to ask them what they're smoking! Seriously though, any informed businessperson knows that few people take action on the basis of seeing (or hearing) only one ad. This question will help you accurately identify if the advertiser understands the principles of basic marketing. You've heard about the magic rule of seven, right? Back in the old days, seven times was the number of times people needed to see an ad before they took action from that ad. In today's streaming, texting, multi-tasking, googling, facebooking society, that number has jumped to 20 or more. If you're dealing with an advertiser who thinks people will take action on the basis of seeing just one ad one time, you will have an opportunity to enlighten him/her with facts. Providing good examples by sharing success stories from other advertisers will help in this situation.

Tell your advertiser about the story of a guy who needed to have his roof repaired, so he's looking in the newspaper for a roof repair service. The likelihood of finding the ONE ad the AAA Roof Repair Company ran three months ago is slim and none. However, if Smith's Expert Roofing Company runs an ad every month in the local paper, his chances of getting the business are far greater than the one-ad wonder. And of course, if Smith's Expert Roofing also has a user-friendly website, uses Google Ad Words, and runs on radio, he has increased his chances of getting the business exponentially.

So, if you are working with the advertiser who thinks they can advertise only once, you can suggest they reduce the size of the big ad and run several times a year with smaller ads because ad frequency is so important. Now you're really into the mode of helping your advertiser and working with them to overcome their objections.

The bigger point that the advertiser needs to understand is that to be a success they need to advertise in multiple ways on multiple days.

Question #3: *"How much would the perfect marketing plan cost you per month?"* The purpose of asking this question is to learn how much your advertiser is willing to invest in advertising to increase their business. For the most part, advertisers know precisely what their monthly budget is, but you'll occasionally hear a response like, "*I don't know.*" When that happens, I'll try this follow-up question, "*Well then, what price range would make you comfortable, whether it's with me or somebody else? Because the only way I can help you grow your business is to know what type of investment you're willing to make to grow your business.*" Then, share a success story of from one of your advertisers.

Question #4: "*Are there any new products or services you will debut in the next six months? Let's plan ahead together.*" Advertisers who have new products, services or specials that actively change are great, because you can go back to them regularly. It's so much better to have an advertiser like this than one who is stagnant!

As a proactive, professional sales executive you should be tracking or monitoring your advertisers' activity in the area of new product and/or service announcements. One of the best ways to do this is to utilize Google Alerts. Once created, your Google Alerts will email you with news about the new product and/or services of the company (advertiser) you specified.

Question #5: "*Do you have a system in place to track your advertising?*" With this question you can determine if your advertiser is using any method to track response from the advertising they have done. Ask them about dedicated call-in numbers, special promo codes, unique web sites, unique URL's, coupons, etc. Surprisingly, the majority of advertisers do NOT track the response. If you find that's true for your advertiser, that might be a strategic point you can address during your sales call, especially if your company offers any kind of assistance in ad response tracking.

Question #6: *"How does social media play a role in your advertising?"* This is a great question because it allows you to talk about the areas in which your company is involved. And, you will find out how much they really know about social media. Because it's still relatively new, a lot of companies are using social media, but it's the absolutely wrong place for them! Their demographics don't match their Facebook page and the reach isn't there. But somebody told them to post it to save money. Don't misunderstand, social media is awesome, but it's just one part of the overall marketing mix. Asking this question will enable you to provide advice on the use and ramifications of social media.

Question #7: *"What ads have worked for you in the past and why? What ads didn't work for you and why?"* This question allows you to determine if your products might be a good fit for the advertiser. If the ads they've run in the past have worked and your products have a similar demographic, you can suggest that your advertiser run the ads with you and double their success. On the other hand, if the ads didn't work for the advertiser, you need to discover the reasons why so you won't repeat the same mistakes in any future ads they run with you. These types of open-ended questions will better provide you with a gauge to determine your advertiser's expectations and allow you to prepare your proposal accordingly.

Advertisers frequently stick with the ads they are running, even if they're not successful, thinking the ads will work eventually. Based on this question, you want your advertiser to know that you're there for them if their current advertising isn't working out. You want them to call you!

I also like to suggest the idea of taking with you ad samples to show success to clients. For example, my magazine sales people have a binder filled with great full page and half page ads. My television reps have great TV spots on their tablets, phones or a thumb drive they can leave behind.

Question #8: *"What can I do as a sales person to make you happy?"* I like to be personal and get down to the nitty gritty. If they do not know, I often prime the situation by offering the following ideas.

SELLING BACKWARDS • 97

1. How do you like me to communicate with you?
    Phone or email?
2. What time of day is best for me to call you?
3. If I bought you lunch every month would you like
    that?
4. Do you like to see three sample ads or is one
    enough?
5. What type of new ideas do you favor? Digital,
    print, events?

Remember, client happiness is critical. You've probably experienced the advertiser who is never happy, regardless of what they run, where they run, how much
they run and how much they spend. An advertiser who
is unhappy typically tells ten to twelve people. A happy
advertiser might tell only two people, and one of them
will probably not be you. These types of open-ended
questions will help you better gauge what would make
your advertiser happy.

Question #9: *"Who do you feel does a great job marketing in our local market? Who do you feel does a great job
marketing in your industry?"* Or, *"How do you out-perform
your competition?"* I like this question as it gives me a gauge as

to how in touch the client is with the marketing landscape around him/her.

Question #10: *"Tell me how your website plays a role in your marketing efforts?"* I like to ask this question to get some details on how much attention the client is paying to web leads versus phone leads or walk in traffic. This also allows me to be prepared to talk about our digital advertising products that are designed to drive web traffic.

So, what are your 10 critical questions? Do you need 10? There is no magic in the number 10. This is just a guide to get you started. Often I will only ask three or four questions on a sales call. The idea is that you are gathering data to be able to customize your presentation to the clients' exact needs. Get started on your critical questions today. They are a very important part of the total sales call and the total *Selling Backwards Sales Process.*

Ok, so you have asked some great questions and took good notes. Now, let's start our pitch (or presentation).

Phase #5 of the sales meeting: Offering your products or solutions only after you understand their needs, goals and desires.

Phase #5 and #6 go hand in hand. So, let's start phase #5 with a clear understanding of our goal in this phase. It would be awesome if we could always meet with the decision maker. Right? Ok, we all know that we meet with marketing directors or one side of a partnership about 90% of the time. So you are going to be pitching to the marketing director or agency media buyer which is absolutely ok. But you must understand, even if you're told otherwise, most marketing directors are not the final decision-makers.

Knowing that, your actual job is to...

1. Make the meeting memorable.
2. Make them feel that you were listening to them.
3. Offer solutions based on what you learned from them.
4. Use strong visuals to get your points across.
5. Provide simple points that are easy to understand.
6. Provide them sales material that they can take to their boss for final approval.

We want to make sure that our pitch or presentation appears to be customized for the client. We do not want to come across as generic in any way. We accomplish this by using the information we have learned from asking our 10 critical

questions and making sure that we also weave into the presentation the answers or success stories that help us answer the
issues raised in the 5 factors covered with the sales consideration funnel.

It is very common to hear a sales person mention that
they have been "perfecting their pitch." Or, they have been
"practicing their presentation." What I preach against is the
one-sided pitch or one-sided presentation. No one, I mean NO
ONE likes to hear a generic sales pitch. Do you? If so, head to
Florida and sit in a timeshare presentation. They are the
worst! So to that end, it is critical that your pitch not be one-
sided; it should be perceived as customized by the person to
whom you're speaking. You truly want the sales pitch to be all
about the advertiser or client.

Ok, looking back at your notes when you created your
10 critical questions, there are probably some answers that
stand out as important to mention. That gives you a starting
point for your pitch. If you are inclined or required to use a
prepared Power Point, you can still customize the presentation,
but it is harder to do so. So, let's assume you do not have to
customize. (By the way, the fastest way to kill a sales call is to
pull out a Power Point presentation!)

Ok, so let's say you have four ideas to pitch. As you talk about each idea you marry that idea with a success story of another client that is happy using the idea. Do not use words like *"They tried this and liked it."* Instead, say things like *"Ron Reynolds found this idea to be one of the best of his year."* Then, explain the idea. Give enough detail to get your point across, but do not lose your advertiser in the details. Then, after you share the idea, it is CRITICAL that you use this phrase, *"How I think this will help your business is…"*. Then, explain why and how you think this idea will benefit them.

To summarize: As we move into Phase #6, you want the conversation to be all about them. You want to incorporate into the conversation the answers the advertiser provided you from the questions you asked. Then, begin to move on to the next phase of the sales call. Phase #6 is all about the visual aids you will use as you make your pitch effective.

Phase #6 of the sales meeting: Offering an on-site proposal by using visually rich one-sheets and pricing grids.

When I leave a sales call, my goal as a sales person is to insure the advertiser will have what they need in order to make a decision. Sometimes you will need to create a custom proposal. I hope that is not the case 75% of the time. In most cases, what I present and how I present it are sufficient for a decision. Having to go back to the office to write an entirely new proposal is a huge waste of my time. And time is money, right? Many of you cannot or will not sell off pricing grids and visual one sheets. No problem. For this reason I have devoted the next chapter of this book to proposals. For now, stay with me and prepare to learn my strategy that has increased revenue 25% for most of my media clients and they DO NOT have to write a custom proposal. When I am done, the client will have what they need to make a decision.

Equipping the marketing director to go to his/her boss is a simple matter of providing relevant and succinct material that can be presented at a later date. PERIOD!

The information should be provided in the form of THREE single one sheets that you can present during your pitch, and leave with your advertiser. An example of each is shown at the end of the book.

1. **A data sheet:** This single sheet explains in simple detail about your audience, readerships, demos, etc. In addition some details about your media in general; position in the market, years in business, etc. It is very visual and contains no more than <u>10 bullet points</u>. Each data

sheet should contain information relevant to the advertiser to whom you are talking. For example, you would have a data sheet specific to restaurant owners and maybe one for lawyers, etc. (Again, an example of this sales sheet is shown at the end of the book.)

2. **An "At a glance offerings" sheet:** This is again a highly visual sheet that shows the advertiser all the things that you have to offer in a very simple way. I like to think of it as a spoke and wheel drawing.

3. **A pricing grid:** This is where the rubber meets the road. This is grid that shows the pricing of your advertising packages in a simple format.

Notice that I did not mention a media kit. Hmmm. Why not? Media kits are not used by my sales teams in any way, shape or form. As a matter of note, I preach against media kits because they are generic and lack focus. They attempt to cover every base and are often prepared by a non-sales person.

Start your pitch by presenting your data sheet. Note on the example's right hand side, there are ten pieces of data that are relevant to the advertisers' market. For example, if you were calling on a restaurant, you would want readership stats and information related to *restaurants*, not plumbers.

The data sheet should include graphic images that are of good quality and intuitive to understand. Best-selling author and sales guru Chet Holmes discusses the importance of using visuals during a sales call in his book, *Ultimate Sales Machine.* Why? Because 86% of people are visual learners. That means 86% of people gain knowledge and understanding through explicitly visual tools. Knowing this fact, why would you NOT use visuals? Think back to grammar school... visuals were an integral part of your initial learning process as a child.

Because advertisers frequently don't understand the depth and breadth of your audience, your data sheet should include a graphic image or picture that represents the size of your audience. For example, you can tell your advertiser dozens of times that your products are read by 35,000 affluent homeowners in the Dallas/Fort Worth market, but they still won't completely understand. Show them a picture of fans on the front stretch of the Texas Motor Speedway, and say... *"We are read by more people that you could fit on the front stretch of the Texas Motor Speedway!"* You'll probably hear, *"Wow! That's a lot of people!!"* A picture is worth 35,000 words.

During a sales call, place your data sheet on the desk, turn it around and slide it right under the nose of the marketing manager for her review. Verbally walk him/her through the facts at a comfortable pace, allowing for questions. You won't believe how effective this will be! Be sure to ask often if the advertiser/client understands what you are sharing. I actually say, "Does this all make sense? If not, please let me know and I will offer more detail." I always want the client to be very comfortable asking questions. You can also say, "What questions do you have so far for me. No question is to simple or to large." The advertisers comprehension of what you are sharing is paramount to getting the deal signed. Remember, people do not buy what they do not understand.

If you are making a sales call by phone, ask your advertiser if you can send the data sheets via email, so they can review them during your phone meeting. (Advertisers appreciate this, as it saves them the hassle of taking notes.) Verify your advertiser receives the email before you go on with your sales pitch, and then walk them through the details.

The second sheet you should present to your advertiser is the "At a glance" overview of your offerings. It visually depicts everything you can offer to your advertiser. Place the title of your main property i.e., magazine name, television or radio station etc., in the center of the page. Then, like the spokes of a wheel, place all of the services/offerings you can provide for your advertiser around the center picture.

Your offerings sheet will allow you to explain the details of your product offerings to your advertiser during your sales call. This practice really helps your advertiser understand just how helpful your products can be to their business. And, this tool is an awesome way to keep the conversation on track. Remember; do not overwhelm the sheet with text. Keep it simple.

The third sheet you have for your sales call is your pricing grid. I don't care what media you're in, integrated packaging works. Period! Packaging sets the tone of the product. When advertisers are considering what media to purchase, the packaging of your offerings can greatly influence their decision.

Years ago, McDonalds initiated a new concept that fundamentally increased their revenue by 300% annually. Instead of selling their products individually, they started offering "Value Meals," "Happy Meals" and other bundles, resulting in instant success; the concept has been copied by businesses of all kind, because it produces results. McDonalds didn't change <u>what</u> they were selling-- by packaging their products differently, they made it easier for the customers *to buy* what they were selling!

If you do a little market research on your own, you'll find examples of price bundling just about everywhere you look. Some bundled products save the consumer only pennies, but the consumer makes the purchase because of perceived value. The companies rely on a little psychology to make consumers <u>think</u> they're saving money. Companies rely on price bundling to increase sales, because when purchasing a bundled product, consumers tend to purchase more than they would have otherwise.

In the pricing grids I create and present, I actually do save my advertisers money. I want them to know the more traditional media they buy from me, the more I can do for them in the digital space. I want them to understand how buying massive multi-media from me can save them tons of money.

In today's environment, ways to advertise via media continues to expand rapidly. It's important that you keep your pricing grid fresh, adding any new digital opportunities. And it's even more important to keep your pricing grid simple and relevant, making it easy for your advertiser to buy multi-media from you.

By creating a pricing grid with strong visuals, you're going to have a powerful tool that will help your advertiser make a decision in your favor. Remember, just like the other two sheets, you want to slide this sheet under the nose of the marketing director (or email, if the sales call is by phone). Providing your information in an easy-to-understand format is so critical to the success of your sales call. And by leaving your three sheets with your advertiser, you're providing them with tools they will use when taking your proposal forward to the ultimate decision maker.

One thing I'd like to caution you about, and this is very important: Never, ever, EVER send follow-up information after your pitch. (Of course, you might send the proposal, but that is NOT the same as follow-up information.) At the end of your pitch, do NOT say, "Thanks for your time, and listen, I'll send you some follow up information." By saying this, you're sug- gesting the sales call was incomplete. Likewise, do NOT send an email containing follow-up information, because guess what...that email will be lost and/or not read. Guaranteed! Now, sometimes you will need to gather info based on a ques- tion the client asks. I get that. What I am saying is that if you can, present what is applicable on the spot. Notice I used the word "applicable". Do not present everything you have. This is called "flooding". No-one likes a flood.

With my method, you'll present your information to your advertiser LIVE, one time, whether in person or via phone. Your information will be so clear and so relevant there is no need to follow up with a proposal! You'll be able to immediately assess whether your advertiser comprehends your pitch or needs more clarification.

What about using iPads during your live pitch? Many of you have bosses who are now insisting you use an iPad or laptop to present your pitch. I love technology as much as the next guy, but I ask that you put yourself in your advertisers' shoes. Pretend you're a marketing director and you have agreed to a sales call. In walks the ad sales executive with his iPad. *"Oh no!,"* you're thinking. *"How long is this going to take?"* The sales executive then places the iPad on your desk and begins the pitch. If you're lucky, he/she places the device in a position where you can actually see the screen, and they are skilled enough to walk you through the information without hovering over your shoulder. More often than not, the sales executive talks too much and too quickly, and you are unable to follow their succinct points on the screen. Even worse, you are forced to take notes, which you have to use later to make the decision with the decision maker. This whole process annoys you and gives you an easy reason to say no.

Can you see how much better it would be for a marketing director if the sales executive asked critical, thought-provoking questions, followed by productive exchange of ideas, finishing with three, well-formatted pages which included intuitive graphics, succinct facts and logical flow?

If you simply must create custom written proposals, the next chapter will cover how I would write the very best proposals for maximum impact!

Phase #7 of the sales meeting: Handling Objections and Setting a time for next steps.

After presenting my three one sheets, I will ask for further questions and then ask for the order. It is amazing to me the number of sales people that are afraid to ask for the order. Then, I set a time to follow-up. Ok, before we tackle the follow-up, let's talk about the three most common objections that occur at the end of the sales call.

1. I don't have any money.

2. My budget is allocated already.

3. I need to talk to my partner.

You will occasionally have an advertiser tell you they simply don't have ANY budget. When this happens I will ask them, *"Does that mean you don't have any budget for ME, or you simply don't have any budget at all?"* I make it very clear. If they have no budget at all, I'll share some success stories of people who have run with me, and will detail some results of the ads that were ran. I will also try to find out if they like the idea. I would say, *"Ok, if money is not the issue, do you like the idea?"* I would try to get their agreement on the idea and then ask them what the campaign would need to cost to make a deal happen.

Another response you might hear is the advertiser saying they don't have any money left in the their budget, yet you know they're advertising with someone else. Now I'll ask, *"Does that mean you don't have any money left for ME, or you simply don't want to run any ads with us. I see that you're running on Channel 7. Is that ad working?"* I want to discover when their current advertising campaign ends, and if it has been successful. I want to learn what I need to do to be their next choice for marketing. Also, I would try to get a vote of confidence on the idea. Another approach to this common objection is to say, "If you would be so kind, please tell me why the 25,000 readers of my magazines are not important to you." This puts the advertiser on the hot seat. Some one you will not be bold enough to ask this question. COME ON! Step up your game people. Be kind. Be sincere. Just ask it!

What about the dreaded, *"I need to talk to my partner."* AHHHH! I want to scream. I would first get a vote of confidence on the idea. Do they like the idea? Then, I would ask for a time that I could present the idea to the partner. If that is not an option then I would be sure to set up a way for them to contact me quickly, normally via cell phone, if the partner has questions. I would also ask how likely it is their partner will like the idea. I would also ask if there is anything else they need from me to close the deal with the partner.

The final step is setting a time for follow-up. Since most business people use their smart phones to manage their calendar, I like to ask them to get out their calendars and get a follow-up meeting synced up. It is a very telling detail if they refuse to do this. If they refuse, I would simply ask them if they need more information or if they really did not like the idea. I would allow them to tell you if they do not like the idea. You do not have to be pushy. You can just be forward. *"You seemed to like the idea. I don't want to be one of those sales people that annoy you by calling you 100 times to follow-up.* (wink,wink) *So, if you truly don't like the idea and don't want me to follow up, please tell me now. You will not hurt my feelings."* This is not rude. This is ideal. Get comfortable with this approach and own the situation!

The final phase of the *Selling Backwards Sales Process* is so critical that Chapter 6 of this book is dedicated to follow-up. Your ability to follow-up with a passion is critical to your sales success. For now, let's get comfortable knowing that we now have a plan of attack that we can follow for our next sales call that will increase our chances of success.

Now, before we leave this chapter on hosting great meetings, it is important to note that many of you cannot or will not choose to sell off of pricing grids. No worries, mate. For this reason I have devoted the next chapter of this book to proposals.

I'm going to end this chapter the way I began, and that's talking about the sales consideration funnel. Remember that each time you make a sales pitch in front of an advertiser, they are going to be asking themselves five questions. They will wonder if your products and services are going to make

them money. What's in it for THEM? They're going to wonder
if you, as their ad sales rep, will be there for them? They'll be
thinking about the content and the format of their ad, and
worrying about the ad's creative to-dos. They'll consider
whether the ad will make them look good to their boss. And
finally, they will be deciding if they like the idea and price of
the ad.

To answer these questions rolling around in the advertiser's head, you need to be prepared to share success stories
for each of the objections or roadblocks. Answer a question
with another question, which will lead to more discussion.
Your job is to make is easy for the advertiser to say "Yes!" You
do that by overcoming those objections and roadblocks.

Hosting sales calls is not rocket science and basically
anybody can do it. However, hosting *great* sales calls requires
a good process, helpful aids, great communication skills (that
includes listening more than talking!) and finally and perhaps
most importantly – practice. We all know how to get to Carnegie Hall, right? Practice, practice and practice!

The best ad sales executives I know spend the time it
takes THEM to get it right. They practice with their spouse,
their partner, their kids or work peers. They record themselves

with a video camera. They practice in a mirror. They practice until they can nail it, resulting in sales calls that progress smoothly, efficiently and professionally. One thing they never do is practice on their advertisers!

Let's say you hired a caterer to prepare a special meal for an important event in your life. At the appointed time and place, the caterer arrives and begins preparations, but in minutes you can tell she isn't sure of herself, she isn't confident and she stammers and stutters when you ask questions. The meal eventually gets prepared, but the experience was far below your expectations. Would you hire the caterer again? Would you recommend them to a friend? More than likely you would not. If you practice on your advertiser, he/she is going to feel just like you did when that mediocre caterer arrived. Brooks Robinson once said, *"If you're not practicing, somebody else is, and he'll be ready to take your job."*

Ok, let's take a look at how to create killer proposals in the next chapter.

CHAPTER FIVE

Presenting great proposals, Keeping it simple.

I n this Chapter, I want to share ten tips for creating great ad sales proposals. Please keep in mind that I most often sell media using the pricing grids detailed in chapter four and shown at the end of the book. With that said, many of you choose or are required to use written proposals due to your current business sales model. I would challenge you to consider moving to a more efficient, less customized proposal model. But, because it is very common for me to coach sales teams through their written proposals, this is a very critical chapter in the total *Selling Backwards Sales Process* as it means you are nearing the end of the total sales process. What is interesting to me is that many sales people feel that the proposal is the final stage in the sales process. This is not only wrong, but dangerous. So, let's dig in together.

Step #1: Understanding What the Proposal Represents.

Step #2: Keep Your Proposals Simple.

Step #3: Always Include An Executive Summary.

Step #4: Keep Your Proposals Two Pages or Less.

Step #5: Scan the Proposal For Clarity.

Step #6: What is Your Differentiating Factor?

Step #7: Pushing Frequency Is Critical.

Step #8: Setting A Deadline For The Deal.

Step #9: Getting the Proposal Signed.

Step #10: Relentless Follow-up.

Step #1: Understanding What the Proposal Represents. The first thing I want to point out in this chapter is the fact that advertisers buy *results*, not proposals. Even if an advertiser says that they are looking for exposure or branding, results are always expected. If you feel like the proposal is the deciding factor in the advertiser's decision-making process, you are just way off the mark. The proposal should just be a wrap up, or a summary of what you want your advertiser to purchase from you. Because many ad sales reps mistakenly believe the proposal is the deciding factor, they don't put a lot of emphasis in the educational process during the sales call. This is a mistake that will cost in terms of lost revenue.

Step #2: Keep Your Proposals Simple. Do you remember the phrase, *"You had me at hello."* This phrase was popularized years ago by the movie *Jerry Maguire.* At the end of the movie, when Jerry expresses his love in a long-winded speech to Dorothy, Dorothy's reply was the simple phrase: *"You had me at hello."* The reason I want you to remember this is important. Often, you will have the advertiser ready to buy your media offerings like a fish on the hook, and then you provide too much detail, and they get confused. In any sales cycle, confusion equals NO! No matter how good the proposal is the advertisers will not buy from you if they don't fully and accurately understand what it is that you are selling. Advertisers do not buy what they do not understand. Period.

It is important to know that when people understand the value of a product they will pay more. For example, an educated car buyer will pay more for a Lexus® even though they know it is actually a high end Toyota®. So, stating the value in your proposal is critical, but doing this often requires a ton of explanation. Thus, the proposal goes from simple to sophisticated. The simplicity of your proposal will seal the deal. No one wants to read a book when presented a proposal. Keep it simple to increase understanding. By nature, most people are averse to taking risks. So, your ability to use a proposal to create a simple, clear understanding in the mind of your advertiser is critical. Again, confusion equals no.

If you agree that confusion equals no, then you'll understand the importance of presenting a proposal that is crystal clear from an educational perspective. That is, your proposal explains what the advertiser is going to receive from you, and what it is going to cost them. But, be careful when explaining the proposal that you don't take a simple proposal and complicate it with details that are not important. For example, I was recently on a sales call where the advertiser was very excited about the multi-media package that the ad sales executive was offering. It was simple and contained four items; print, a banner ad, a Facebook® mention and an eNewsletter ad. The advertiser was ready to sign. Then, the sales person began to explain all the intimate details of the banner ad campaign. He went on to mention the banner ad impressions and the creative. Then, he talked about the click through rate. The advertiser went from buyer to flyer. Meaning, the advertiser flew out the door. NO SALE! The sales person, who "had the advertiser at hello" then proceeded to kill the deal with too many details during the decision-making phase.

Many of you may feel that you need to give the advertiser every detail for fear that the advertiser will be unhappy later. Very rarely have I seen this to be the case. I'm sure every reader of this book has at least one story of an advertiser that was sold one thing and thought another. Advertiser confusion is common, and in fact is an epidemic. But keep in mind that dragging an advertiser into the deep details can kill a deal. So be careful to be clear, but keep your approach as simple and straightforward as possible. In an effort to keep the proposal simple, once you've finished creating your proposal, go back through it and remove every ounce of fluff you've included --unnecessary, ambiguous or redundant information. Remove anything that is not critical to the advertiser's decision-making process. Don't include statistics, charts, facts and figures unless they are critical. This is a proposal, not a media kit. This doesn't mean your pricing grid shouldn't have graphics, nice colors and images, if you choose to use your pricing grid as part of the proposal. But if your proposal includes graphs, charts and figures, it typically is just overwhelming and confusing to the advertiser. Often sales reps include these things "just in case." The educational process should have taken place during the sales call *before* the proposal was presented. So keep it simple if you want to win! The reason I use predetermined packages and pricing grids is because of the numerous issues I am attempting to clarify in this chapter. But, many of you just cannot or will not adopt the predefined grid model. Not an issue, let's roll forward.

Step #3: Always Include An Executive Summary.

Behavioral experts whom I've interviewed have shared a couple of great insights with me. The first one is about the habits of executives and business owners. When presented with a proposal of any kind, the majority of business owners will read only the first and last paragraph, and skim over the contents in the middle. For this reason, it's extremely important to include an executive summary at the <u>beginning</u> of your proposal.

Some sales ad executives wrongly believe that the executive summary should summarize the contents of the proposal. As a result, they write the executive summary last, after all the information has been gathered into the body of the proposal. But think about it...an executive summary is not supposed to summarize the proposal; it's supposed to summarize the reasons why the customer should buy from you. The executive summary should therefore focus on basic issues and bottom-line results—and it should be written first, in order to set the tone and direction of the body of the proposal. Plus, since we know that the executive will probably only read the first and last paragraph, then let's lead with success.

For example, "The goal of this marketing plan is to expose the XYZ Brand to 35,000 affluent readers in the next 3 months. We will do this through an affordable blend of multimedia options that include gorgeous print advertisements and social media ads designed to drive new traffic to your web site. We offer a cost effective way to make this happen that is ROI focused." I would highly suggest that you create several executive summary templates. Tweak and perfect these until you find one that works very well.

Step #4: Choose the Best Format for Your Situation. There are three main types of proposals; package grids, spreadsheets and written formats. Each one has merits. Just like each advertiser is unique, each proposal format serves a purpose. Again, examples of all of these formats are shown at the end of this book.

Format #1: Package grid format: Some of you may choose to use a packaged grid as your proposal, and that's great. A lot of my ad sales strategy clients prefer this method because they feel their pricing sheet has all the pertinent information. They like the strong visuals and/or their pricing grid includes the pricing. Those are all good reasons and they find success with that type of proposal. The idea behind the pricing grid is to showcase all that your multi-media proposal has to offer in a very graphic and easy to understand format. Also this format has a lot more focus on total value and showing discounts.

You may be old enough to recall when many of the major fast food brands launched their "value meal" menu program. Rather than buy a burger, fries and a drink separately , you were prompted to order a #2 or #3. Did you know that most "value menu" items do not actually save you money? In some cases the price of the value meal was the exact same as when you buy all three items on their own. What these fast food restaurants accomplished was to make it easier for you to buy from the menu. Further to this point, they up-sold you into buying items that you may not have even considered. When I am creating pricing grids I use this same philosophy to drive my pricing grid. I have included several proposal examples at the end of the book. I would say that package grid format is by far the most popular and most successful format used for proposals. Keep in mind, if you present a package grid, you frequently avoid returning to the office to create a proposal because the package grid itself is the proposal. Using this format shortens the sales cycle dramatically.

Format #2: Spreadsheet format: This proposal format works well when you are trying to create a yearly media buy and want to show the advertiser all of the details of what they are getting from you each month. You list the months along the top of the spreadsheet and then you detail in columns what each media choice contains. This can be a very effective format if you are working with an advertiser who wants a TON of detail. It is important to really understand what type of advertiser you are talking to when choosing this format. I refer to the advertiser who likes a ton of detail as Data Diane or Data Dave. They love data, stats, figures and want all kinds of details. I would say that this type of advertiser is the minority.

Most advertisers do not read, they scan. Most CEO's only read the first few sentences and skip immediately to the last thing in the proposal.. the price.

If you are creating proposals that are longer than one or two pages, you are probably regurgitating a lot of the discussion that occurred during the sales call. A long, detailed proposal will be confusing to your advertiser, and is counterproductive to your goal. If your proposal is filled with too many details and too much information, the marketing director and/or the owner will not be able to process all the information. Remember, confusion equals NO! If you can whittle your proposal down to just one page, you are right on target.

Another insight I learned from behavior experts is the value of using bulleted points in your proposal, rather than long sentences. When people read bulleted points, rather than long, detailed sentences, their comprehension level goes up exponentially. And using bulleted points makes your proposal less cluttered, much shorter and easier to read.

As mentioned before, the proposals I prefer are on <u>one</u> page and include an executive summary at the top, which includes an ROI focus. The summary of the campaign is next, written in the form of bulleted points. Next, I like to give two or three multi-media options. Last is the price. I want to make it easy for the final decision-maker to comprehend what it is I'm offering without any confusion of his/her part. I want to make it easy for them to say yes.

Whichever method you use for your proposal, be mindful that all proposals should be TWO pages or less. If you can't reduce your proposal to two pages or less, even if you're selling a massive media package, something is off the mark. You're including too much information, too many details and/or too many visuals. Confusion really does equal NO.   Put yourself in your advertiser's shoes. Would you rather be given a six-page proposal filled with long sentences, redundant information and confusing statistics, or a clean, easy-to-read, relevant one-page proposal? I think the answer is very clear.

Step #5: Scan the Proposal For Clarity. Have a business associate or another person on your sales team scan your finished proposal for comprehension. Quiz them after they read it to see if they understood your main points, your offerings and your price. Remember that most CEOs and business owners will scan your proposal and hit the high points; they're basically looking to determine if your stated proposal is (a) what you spoke about in your meeting and (b) truly meets their needs. I know there are many of you who feel this is an unnecessary step, so you won't take the time to complete it.   However, for those of you who really, fervently want to improve your selling skills, for those of you who are going to do whatever it takes to become the best ad sales executive in the office, this step is mission critical! It's very important to listen to your peer's feedback. If he/she doesn't understand the points of the proposal, how on earth can you expect your advertiser to get it? You're seeking to get your advertiser to do something, to accept your written plan for completing a task, which is advertising with you. Rewrite your proposal until that objective is met and you will be ready for the next step. Proposal writing should not be taken lightly.

If every advertiser accepted your proposal immediately upon reviewing it, you wouldn't need my last tips. In the real world, advertisers often times need a nudge or two. That's why my next tip is important.

Step #6: What is Your Differentiating Factor? I'd like you to think about this: What is the differentiating factor that makes you different or better than your competition? What is your "D FACTOR"? How are your products different from and/or better than the next guy's? Maybe your products are the number one position in your market. Maybe they are a solid number three or four in the market. Maybe you are the differentiating factor, and you are the reason the advertiser should advertise with you. Whatever it is, be prepared to state this clearly to the advertiser in your proposal.

It is important to understand that price becomes the deciding factor when your products appear similar to your competitor. You may want to state this in your executive summary or at the end near the price. Because proposing is about persuading, think about what you can say to convince your advertiser to say yes to your proposal. For example, "We are read by more affluent business owners than all other magazines combined in the Houston market." Or, "We are the only web site that is used by over 75% of all members of the Chicago Small Business Alliance." It is critical that you show-case your differentiating factor in your proposal. If you do not do this, price might become a much bigger factor in the deci-sion-making process. Remember, price becomes the deciding factor when you and your competitors seem similar. So the differentiating factor you state will help fight against the price comparison issues. It won't solve the price debate, but it will help.

Step #7: Pushing Frequency Is Critical. Your sales calls and proposals should focus on helping your advertiser under-stand that they need to advertise on multiple days and in mul-tiple ways. State this – learn this – memorize it, because it's so important. *"To be competitive in today's marketing jungle, you need to advertise on multiple days in multiple ways."* During your sales calls and in your proposal, you should men-tion and reinforce it, because that is the beauty and essence of multimedia. By utilizing multimedia, your advertiser can reach a similar audience in various ways. State this in your proposal and list out the options. Carry the 'multiple days/multiple ways' option throughout all of your communications with your advertiser. Remember, most advertisers do not understand frequency pricing or frequency pricing grids. So do not rely on them from your media kit to sell the advertiser. Do not place frequency pricing grids from your media in your proposal.

Instead, I like to show the discount that they will receive in red. For example, in the proposal I will show a rate of $1500. This is the one-time rate. If they run three times the rate drops to $1,000. I will show them the frequency discount in red of $500 and show the $1,000 rate below. It is critical that you show the discount and not assume the advertiser understands the frequency discount. Even better, list a rate and then offer a stated discount like 15% more off if the advertiser runs more than one month. You can also be creative with your pricing and offer a free ad for every three that they buy. All in all, very often creative pricing wins out before deep discounts.

The problem I often observe is that sales managers and sales people often make it very complicated to buy an ad. Because some of you have been selling ads for years you often forget that buying an ad is a big complicated decision for most advertisers. What is even more interesting is that when I point this out, most media executives don't believe me. Most media pricing is not easy to understand and this complication often leads to confusion on the part of the advertiser. When advertisers don't understand, they don't buy.

Step #8: Setting A Deadline For The Deal. Always include some kind of deadline in your proposal. Perhaps you offer your advertiser some kind of discount, say 10-15%, and have a deadline attached to the discount. The deadline is specific to your proposal, not an internal deadline. I typically have a deadline of one week. The purpose of having a deadline is to add an incentive and a little bit of urgency to their decision-making process. I've found this technique effective in getting a timely response back from the advertiser. A note of caution here for print media sales people: DO NOT make the deadline of the proposal the same as the deadline of the publication. This adds a level of stress that is not needed. Be cautious about using your publication deadline to force action of your advertisers' part. They do not want to hear, *"Hey Tom, my publication deadline is Friday, could I have your decision today?"* That technique can work well, but you do not want to stack up all your proposals in that way as you will have a log jam that is often hard to manage and truly not needed.

I have some clients that offer a signing bonus to their advertisers. For example, sign up for one year and receive a

$500 Visa gift card. Of course, you have to be sure that this meets the ethical standards of the client you are working with for this to be effective.

Step #9: Getting the Proposal Signed and

Step #10: Relentless Follow-up

These two steps are so important that Chapter 6 of this book is dedicated to their explanation. Hopefully, you had an opportunity to present a pre-determined price grid based package deal that was something that could be signed right on the spot. But what happens often is that the advertiser will ask, *"Can you get back to me with a proposal?"* Or, they *"Love the idea…."*, but just need to run it by their partner or boss. This happens all the time and most sales executives do not handle the situation correctly and then this client will fall into the D-zone. "D" can stand for dead or deleted. Because this step in the *Selling Backwards* process is so important, I have dedicated an entire chapter to the plan of attack. So, let's move on to Chapter 6 for all the details on getting the proposal signed and following up with a passion!

CHAPTER SIX

Getting the proposal signed and never ending follow-up.

J ust in case you skipped right to this chapter, this chapter represents steps #9 and #10 in the proposal process, a very important part of the *Selling Backwards Sales Process.* I would encourage you to back up a chapter and read steps #1- #8 to better understand and increase your chances of sales success.

Here are my 8 best tips to getting a proposal signed:

Tip # 1. Set a time for follow-up during the sales call.

Tip # 2. Create a follow-up pattern.

Tip # 3. Utilize a sales close process.

Tip # 4 Give your client an opportunity to say "No."

Tip # 5. Do NOT negotiate the price against yourself.

Tip #6. You've got to be bold – but you don't need to be brash.

Tip #7: Use an electronic signature tool to get the agreement or proposal signed.

Tip #8: There are other ways to try to get a meeting if the advertiser just goes completely DEAD! (Zero response.)

On all sales calls I coach my clients to always try and present an ad package on the spot and get a signature on the spot. Before you slam this book down saying this will never work, consider this, what if this idea worked only 1% of the time? This is one of those "never hurts to try" type scenarios. Right? Ok, so let's be real, since this does not happen the vast majority of the time, what can we do to get a signature?

I think we all would agree that what happens most of the time, an advertiser will ask you to get back them with a proposal. Or, they love the idea, but just need to run it by their partner or boss. This happens all the time and most sales executives do not handle the situation correctly and then the client falls into the D-zone. "D" can stand for "dead", "dark", "dumb" or "deleted". None of these are good. As we have talked about many times in this book, you need a plan for each stage of the sales process. Setting expectations for follow-up and then the actual follow-up after a client meeting is no different. (See Step #7 on page 102 for a refresh on this issue.)

Tip #1. Set a time for follow-up during the sales call. Before you leave the meeting or hang up the phone, you need to ask them 3 times for an opportunity to follow-up, meaning while you have the client's attention, you are going to say, (before you even agree to a proposal), *"Happy to create a proposal for you. It will take a bit of time. I would like to set a five-minute meeting with you on Thursday at 9am or 2pm to review the proposal. Which would work better for you for a 5 minute chat?"* If the advertiser doesn't agree, you can say, *"I assure you this will only take 5 minutes, How about Friday at 9am or 2pm?"* Or you could say, *"Is there a better time you would like to suggest?"* If I am face-to-face with a client, I will pull out my cell phone and attempt to place the appointment on my mobile calendar. You need to try and set a specific date and time to review your proposal. Do not forget to add the client's email to the meeting invite and set a 30 minute meeting reminder as well.

All throughout this book we have talked about not wasting a client's time. This part of the process is no different. Make a BOLD promise to not waste their time with this follow-up meeting. I often even warn them by saying, "*I don't want to be one of those pesky sales people that calls you 1,000 times after a great meeting like this.*" *(wink)* I think they will get your drift.

It is important to note that if after three attempts to get the client to commit to a proposal follow-up meeting they still say no, you may be dealing with a client that actually does not want a proposal. To that end, I will often pose this question. "*Bob, you will not hurt my feelings if you do not want this proposal. I would rather you tell me now as I value your time and want to be respectful of your time.*" Now, if you are very bold, you could say, "*Bob, do you want to see the same success as the other business owners I have spoken about today? If so, why are you unwilling to set a time to review the proposal I am going to prepare for* you?" Each one of you reading this book has a different style, so you need to take this conversation in the best direction for you and your client. But never be afraid to be bold if you feel like the deal is close to being lost.

Of course, you know what happens sometimes, even if you get an agreement on a date and time. You will call your client or stop by their office at the scheduled time, and they are M.I.A. Missing in action. Gone and nowhere to be found. Don't you hate that? But, it happens. Obviously, you need to get back on their calendar so the first thing you have to do is reach out to the client again. And again! You need to go back to a pattern just like the one you used in the *Big 50 Prospecting Plan.* Experts tell us that after a sales call, even if things go perfectly, you may have to reach out 15 to 20 times to re-engage the client. Why is that and what can you do to shorten that delay?

The "why" is, that people simply get busy and forget or they actually did not want a proposal in the first place. Last minute issues simply come up in a busy office environment and your meeting may get overlooked. In order to help prevent this from happening and to shorten the delay, you can be proactive by setting a time to review the proposal while you are still at your sales call. And prior to the scheduled meeting, use your Outlook or Google calendars to send them reminders. Promising the advertiser by phone or email that you are going to stop by their office helps also. Tell your client you're going to be politely persistent until you get some type of answer.

One thing you should NOT do is give up! Let me share a statistic of mine based on years of coaching clients all over the country: Ninety percent – 90%!!- of all sales people give up after only 4 attempts and most of those attempts are via email. You might say, *"But Ryan – I contact my clients every other day until they give me an answer!"* At the risk of sounding skeptical, I find that hard to believe in most cases. Remember, I have managed and coached literally thousands of media sales reps for years, and I know it as fact – most of them simply give up after three or four attempts. And most of those attempts are via email!

If you are squirming a little bit while reading this, you are probably a wee bit guilty of following up with email the majority of time. It's just easier, right? Yes, it's easier for YOU, but it's simply not effective! Every media sales person uses email. The vast majority, especially younger sales people, stick to email 85% of the time.

For those of you who really do follow up 15-20 times, you're going to have far greater success of actually connecting with your client after repeated attempts. And you are likely to hear something like this: *"Ryan, I'm really sorry I haven't got back to you yet... I was on vacation, and then got slammed when I got back, etc. etc. Man, I just forgot to get back to you!"*

Here's what my experiences have shown. If during the meeting you thoroughly explained your options and left the prospect good collateral that they were able to share with the decision-maker, (plus you determined that they "really" wanted a proposal), the chances of reconnecting with them are very good. However, if you simply droned on and on during your sales call and left no materials (other than your media kit – groan), the chances of reconnecting with this advertiser is marginal. You simply must – MUST- make 15-20 attempts to follow-up with your client after your sales meeting. (Am I being patiently persistent yet?) So, how do you follow up 15-20 times without being a pest?

Tip # 2. Create a follow-Up Pattern: Make it a practice to follow up every other day. Now some of you may by thinking "Every other day?? Isn't that that the very definition of being a pest?" Actually, NO, because at least 50% of your voice mails and emails are going to get deleted! As people check their mobile devices to read emails, they're quite likely to delete any non-critical emails, thinking they will get back to the sender, but then they simply forget to do so.

In my *Big 50 Prospecting Plan*, you learned why using templates for voice and email messages is so effective. Likewise, I highly encourage you to create templates for your follow up voice and email messages when following up after a sales call. I like to have 5 or 6 templates for my follow-up activity. You never, ever want to leave the same voice mail or email twice. You are better than that!

Here's an example of a voicemail: *"Hey Bob, it's Ryan from Hoosier Magazine calling on that proposal you asked me to prepare– I'd love to get it signed so I can get rolling for you. Remember that VIP discount expires tomorrow. Our 35,000 readers will be excited to see your ad, Bob."* The email you send immediately after leaving your voice message is very similar. Keep in mind, in an effort to not be a pest, you need to be polite and you want to be positive. When you leave your voice message, your voice should sound enthusiastic and happy – you can't wait to help your advertiser with his/her promotion!

I observe a lot of sales reps using a technique that I disapprove of—using a deadline as a leverage to get your client to react. *"Hey Bob, I really need to hear back from you about that proposal, as the deadline for ad submission is just a week away!"* I'm sure YOU don't appreciate being pressured, and I can tell you your advertisers hate this technique! After all they are the clients, and they don't HAVE to advertise with you! I once read a quote that fits well here: "Lack of planning on your part does not constitute an emergency on mine!" Selling on a deadline just never produces a positive result! You are the one that is selling to close to the deadline. I truly find that this approach never works well. Let me be clear on this point. I am not saying that deadlines are bad. What I am saying is that often sales executives wait until the last minute to sell media. Because the sales person planned poorly, then the client is placed under a level of pressure that is not fair or helpful.

Tip # 3. Utilize a sales close process. Every single thing you do in sales has to have a process, and closing a deal is no different. Let me provide you with a sports example. A few years ago, I took golf lessons to improve my game. It seemed I was doing things correctly, but the results were not satisfactory. If you know anything about golf, you know that hitting the golf ball consistently is so important – you can hit the ball slightly off (I'm talking centimeters here!) and the ball will go frustratingly off course. My golf instructor told me I needed to develop a perfect "pre-shot process." That's right… a process you execute each time you prepare to swing the club. He told me to practice every little thing I did prior to hitting the ball well, and then commit that routine to memory. Once I had developed and memorized my "pre-shot process," my brain would go on autopilot as I stepped up to the ball and no big surprise – my game improved dramatically! When you can identify a repeatable pattern of success you will see improvement. If you do not create these process based patterns you will always be random. I know of only one instance where ran-domness results in a reward… winning the lottery. For the rest of us… watch out for lightening.

So, what is your sales close process? Do you even have one or do you just walk in blind, and hope they say 'yes' to your proposal? To define and hone your process, think back to the successful closes you've experienced in the past. What steps did you take, and what did you do that contributed to the success? Analyze the steps you took, write them down, and tweak them until you've got it right.

Conversely, what about the times when you just knew you were going to close a big sale, and it flopped. What did you do that might have killed the deal? Was it something you said or did? Stop blaming the client. Look back at all of your processes leading up to the proposal meeting. Are you pros-pecting the right kind of customers? Are you asking insightful questions, and providing the client with relevant information? Are you diligently working your Big 50 Prospect list? See, everything in sales is driven by your processes, and there are steps within each process that should not be skipped over. Don't be guilty of "rolling with the flow." Sales reps that are random in their approach to sales never realize maximum sales success. That is not to say that they will not be successful, they just don't attain the heights reserved for sales superstars.

Tip # 4 Give your client an opportunity to say No. A lot of sales managers jump out of their chairs when they hear this bold statement in one of my workshops. But, let's face it. Sometimes, you're just not going to be able to close the sale, even after all your processes have been worked and you've followed up with the advertisers 15 to 20 times. That's just the reality. When this happens, I use my last resort. I like to give my client the opportunity to say 'no'.

I'm brutally yet politely honest, and I say, *"Hey John, I've followed up with you numerous times. I thought you were really excited about my proposal; if this is just not the right time for this, just please let me know. I'm happy to come back and work with you in another month or so. As you can tell from my numerous calls and emails, I am very excited about you advertising with us. So, if you would be so kind to simply drop me an email I would appreciate it. "* I even explain to my client that as a part of my sales process, I will follow up with them until they give me a 'go' or 'no' response.

Let's face it – if you've really worked your process, and you just can't get the client to respond one way or another, you need to bring the process to a conclusion. It may be that your entire sales process was fine, but for whatever reason, the advertiser simply won't (or can't) commit to your proposal. There may be something going on within their business. It may even be something personal going on in your client's life. If the client's 'no' response is based on price, something you can address, do not negotiate against yourself.

Tip # 5. Do NOT negotiate the price against yourself. Very often, as you experience a client that just isn't willing to close, you start thinking to yourself, *"It must be the price."* So then you start running the various scenarios in your mind and you'll call your client and say, *"Hey Bob, I pitched you that proposal – I thought you really liked it, but you haven't yet given me a go. If it's the price, I'm happy to come down 15-20% if that would get this deal closed."* What I like to say instead is, *"Hey Bob, let me know where that proposal needs to be, price-wise to fit your budget and I'll do my best to work on that. Toss me some budget numbers via email and I will take them to my boss."* This technique avoids the situation where you're negotiating against your self. This tip might help nudge the client from a 'no' decision to a 'go' sale.

Tip #6. You've got to be bold – but you don't need to be brash. There are a lot of sales techniques out there and tons of sales training programs. They are not like mine, or not dedicated specifically to ad sales. Many of them will tell you to try these techniques when you call someone: *"Listen Bob, I'm going to lose my job if you don't call me back."* Or this: *"Hey Susan, I've been calling you repeatedly for a month, and I think it's rude that you aren't returning my calls."* Anytime you throw some negative attitude towards your client, you're going to come across as a typical sales person with a huge ego.

These types of brash responses will result in zero sales and a less than stellar reputation, which is exactly what you do not want. It benefits you to be bold but it always harms you if you come across in a brash and rude manner.

As you are fine-tuning your processes, you need to remember that it's YOUR job to close the sale and not your client's job to do so. So don't give up, follow-up every other day and use your written close process. You should give your client a chance to say "no' and don't negotiate against yourself. Finally—be bold but not brash.

Tip #7: Use an electronic signature tool to get the agreement or proposal signed.

Getting the final signature for approval used to be a bit of a hassle. I'd send the proposal attached to an email, or I would hand deliver the proposal to get a signature. The whole getting-the-signature process took too long and was often very frustrating. Today I use a product from Adobe® called EchoSign®. Like other online signature services, EchoSign® allows me to instantly send my proposal, get an e-sign from the advertiser and then track, file and store my proposal via the web. The program is super easy for me and for my advertiser. I never have to leave my computer or print anything out. And my advertiser never has to scan and/or fax anything back to me. The program is also super cheap! Plus, a great feature of the program is the ability to set and send reminders to your advertiser! I typically will set the program to send a reminder every day when I'm expecting a signature. And it works great for insertion orders too!

Tip #8: There are other ways to try to get a meeting if the advertiser just goes completely DEAD! (Zero response.) Here are a few ideas you might consider as you try and get to a meeting with a client to review the proposal:

1. Call another person at the company to see if your contact is on vacation or out of town on business.
2. Call another sales person at the company you are calling upon and ask for advice in reaching your potential advertiser.

3. Send two pizzas to the office and then follow-up with an email.

4. Send the proposal via snail mail in a priority envelope.

5. Perhaps you are bold enough to just drop into their office. This is not a great idea, but it can work.

6. Tell them via email and voice mail to not feel bad if things have changed. Ask them to just please let you know.

7. Get creative to get the deal. Send flowers, logo cookies, cake.

Ok, let's bring this train back into the station as we close out this topic on getting the deal signed. If you truly feel that the client wanted a proposal, then you need to look carefully at your plan of attack for follow-up. Look back at the last deals you closed and review them in detail. Keep in mind, if you have a sales process it is much easier to track success and failure. Most people think that large automobile manufacturers use an assembly line process simply to increase profits. Nope. The assembly line process also allows the manufacturer to observe quality as well. If a car rolls off the line with a loose wire, they can back track and see where the problem occurred. If you do not have a sales process, it is very hard to see where you might be off track. Remember—randomness kills your sale process. If you want to reach new heights in your sales career, you need to create a winning sales process that allows you to identify repeatable patterns of sales success.

CHAPTER SEVEN

Advertising retention strategies for success.

W ork as hard to keep clients as you did to acquire them and you will have a process for sales success. One of the most important things you need to do as an ad sales rep is to retain your advertisers. Wouldn't you agree that it's a lot easier and certainly more cost effective to retain a customer than to get a brand-new advertiser on board? To that end, what is YOUR strategy for retaining your current advertisers? Many ad sales reps solely rely on their company for this type of program. Would you find it hard to believe that I have never, ever, not even once known a media company that has an actual advertiser retention plan in place? For this reason, if you wait for your company you might be waiting a long time. In addition, since you know that retention is critical, you are missing a very important part of the *Selling Backwards Sales Process.*

So, let's get down to the details. What are you going to do to retain your clients - send Christmas cards? I believe holiday cards are wonderful, but they are a waste of time. If you wait until December to say "thanks" to your customers, a good competitor has beaten you at least 12 times. Your Christmas card will simply be lost in the clutter of all the rest. So if this is your strategy, you have a lot of work ahead of you.

You need to develop a process. (Where have you heard that before?) You need a plan. You need to develop an Advertiser Retention Program, which is going to have 3 components or areas of focus.

Retention Plan Focus Area #1: Monthly Initiatives

Retention Plan Focus Area #2: Quarterly Initiatives

Retention Plan Focus Area #3: Yearly Initiatives

It's more cost effective and less stressful for you if you just create these programs in advance and then let them roll. It's not that difficult to plan, the difficulty is in the ongoing execution of the retention plan.

Retention Plan Focus Area #1: Monthly Initiatives

Let's talk about monthly initiatives and what they look like. I'd like to encourage you to look at monthly email business articles that you can collect and send to your advertisers. How about an email 'thank you' each month, that can be automated? You simply use an automated email provider – set it up in advance at the beginning of the year, and let it work its magic. As you add new advertisers, you simply add them to your email distribution list that automatically goes out on your behalf. How about an email 'thank you' that goes out from the sales manager? How about an email 'thank you' once a year from the publisher? A frequent 'thank you' is something advertisers really appreciate receiving. These emails are easy to do and touch your advertiser in a friendly, more responsive way.

Have you ever considered 'bonus bucks' that add up? Every time an advertiser gets a bill, they get a fifty-dollar bonus buck inside of the bill. Or, purchase some type of promotional item for $4 or less and send it to the advertiser.

Remember in the book, *"The Ultimate Sales Machine,"* when Chet Holmes said, *"These items that you may think are childish are the things that can have a really great benefit. People simply love to get stuff. "* So consider what you can do from a promotional perspective to be able to purchase and send small promotional items embossed with your logo as a thank you to your advertiser. You might be thinking, *"Ryan, I represent a high-end luxury magazine. It's just not something we would do. We'd have to send somebody a Rolex to tell them thank you."* I can't disagree with you more. I have to share this with you—even people in the luxury market absolutely love to be thanked for their participation in your media products.

It doesn't matter what type of media company that you are, advertiser retention is critical. You need a monthly, quarterly and yearly incentive program. You need to do different things each month than you do each quarter and each year. Your 'thank-you' items and actions need to be unique. You need to take care of your advertisers. I have never EVER had anyone say to me, *"You know Ryan, you just thank me too much. You're just too grateful for my business."* Has an advertiser ever, ever said that to you?

Here's an actual scenario to consider. My client is a man named Jim. When I completed the sales process with Jim he was a $6500 client. Not a huge client, but certainly not a small client. I always try to pay specific attention to what the customer likes. So I sent Jim a solar iPad charger. Why? Because he told a story of his iPad always going dead while he flew his small plane on the weekends. Most smaller planes do not have a USB port or a cigarette lighter to use to recharge small electronic devices. Pilots used to use paper maps and now the FAA allows them to use most maps on their iPad. Think about this scenario, if Jim has a choice between me and another account executive, who will he choose? I gave Jim a small gift that shows I really listened to him. Jim is a part of my retention program. He gets a thoughtful gift, monthly re-source content-rich emails, quarterly invites to webinars and parties and yearly retention items too.

Recently while training an ad sales team, I saw the sales manager pass by some gourmet cookies on the table. She mentioned that she followed a rigid gluten-free diet plan. I found some gluten-free cookies online and sent them to her after my visit. Now ask yourself, how does she feel about me now? Do I do this to try and stay close to my clients? Do I do it because I want them to think highly of me, and have a warm and fuzzy feeling about me?

Yes. That's exactly why I do it. I want my customers to think fondly of me. I want to be remembered in a positive way. I want to make sure they won't forget me when they need the services that I offer. I want their repeat business. Retention is critical yet a formalized retention plan is almost never present at the companies who call on me for ad sales help. Sure, certain pieces of a client retention plan might exist, but it is not consistent or long term. So ask yourself: What can I do on a monthly, quarterly and yearly basis to make sure I'm doing as much as possible to retain the advertisers I have worked so hard to get? If your monthly incentive is a thank you note enclosed with their bill, oh my gosh, please just shoot me now. Stop the presses – that is NOT what you want to do. Getting a bill in the mail is NOT the time to thank someone. Why do I use this as an example? Because sales executives tell me they do this all the time! ALL THE TIME! What are the extra things you can do for your advertisers? Are you seen as a resource or are you seen as somebody who just takes their money each and every month? For me, I want to be seen as a resource.

Another part of your monthly retention program should be certain initiatives that prove return on investment to your clients. What is it you are going to do to make sure your advertisers understand the return on investment they have received from buying a marketing program from you? Too many unexplained reports are bad for business. You need to make sure that the accuracy of the reports being presented makes a ton of sense. Make sure the reports are very visual and include good graphics. Overwhelming an advertiser with reports is not necessarily proof of performance – it merely proves that you can generate a report. Anybody can do that. Also any media company can do it—so it's important that you pay careful attention to the reports that you're sending. You should offer to review all the reports with your advertiser. In the report, you want to make sure you include information for all the media that they have purchased from you. Caution—if you don't understand analytics and don't understand the reports that are generated, don't send it to your advertiser. Get your IT person on the phone, make them explain the report to you and educate yourself about the details before you ever pass it on. Otherwise you'll look foolish if your advertiser asks a question which you cannot answer.

Great monthly reports are going to help your advertiser but you have to simplify the reports so your advertiser can understand them quickly. Remember to keep it simple. You want to do the math for them. You want them to understand the exposure numbers. Use a ton of visuals in the report. Don't make your advertiser have to figure out the report. That's YOUR job. Your advertiser may not know the difference between unique users vs total users vs drug users. Use language they will understand and be prepared to explain if they don't. As you're walking your advertiser through the report, keep this in mind—many advertisers are having a difficult time running their own business. How do you expect them to be an expert in media report reading? Let me emphasize and say your report MUST be simple, easy to understand and easy to explain.

Producing monthly reports and reviewing them with your advertisers is such an important part of your retention plan. *"But Ryan,"* you say. *"I send my advertisers a copy of the monthly magazine."* Or, "Ryan, I send them the traffic report from their TV campaign." That's great, I'm thinking. So does every other sales rep out there. What is your differentiating factor? What is it you do differently than every other sales rep out there, which is also going to call on your advertiser this month? Maybe the care you take in presenting this monthly report can be your differentiating factor. Maybe it's the proof in the pudding – the reminder you are there for them.

Retention Plan Focus Area #2: Quarterly Initiatives

Let's talk about quarterly initiatives. How about a 'lunch and learn' series? If you're a city and regional magazine or a local television or radio station, you might be familiar with this concept but you just don't put it into play on a quarterly basis. You actually invite your advertisers to a nice hotel, or someplace you have some trade with, or maybe a nice restaurant. Then, you invite a quality speaker to come in for an hour and give a talk on a topic that would be of interest to your advertisers.

For me, 'lunch and learns' are not all about *selling* as much as they are about *telling*. It gives you a distinct opportunity to have advertisers in a room in a non-sales environment that is non-threatening. In addition, it is important in helping them to better understand marketing based on the topics you present. Remember — an educated advertiser is a good advertiser.

Some of you feel that an educated advertiser is a dangerous advertiser. You may be thinking, *"Ryan, I just don't want an educated advertiser — then they'll know some of the games I try to play with them."* Well, if that's really how you feel about your advertisers, I just don't know how much success you're ever going to be able to achieve. You simply can't grow an advertiser the same way you grow a mushroom—

keeping them in a dark corner, and feed them manure. It's not going to happen. Of course my mushroom analogy is a joke. But there are a lot of implications to it. You've got to keep your advertisers in the light. Communicate, educate and inform them about marketing.

OK, here's an idea for a quarterly incentive: Arrange for one-on-one consults with your strategic partner experts and your advertisers. You will want to create strategic partnerships with local experts to offer these pro level services to your client. Perhaps your strategic partnerships give them access to a social media expert, a sign expert, a graphics expert or someone who does business planning. You might be able to arrange a trade with these experts as well to sweeten the opportunity. Think about different ways you can provide some resources to your advertisers to get them excited about the possibility of doing business with you. You want them to know that if they do business with you, they are going to have access to an expert network at a highly discounted rate. You might be able to go to a local attorney or CPA and say, *"Listen, if I bring some business your way, can you offer them a nice discount for your services?"* Asking the experts does not cost you a thing and the end result is that your customers are going to see you as a valuable resource. Don't over complicate this idea. Some of you need to plan until you see blood. Keep it simple people. Wars are won based on one victory at a time.

I had a sales person that worked for me named Katie. She was a top-level sales person with a ton of local connections to help her clients. She knew a sign guy, a tax guy, a web master, a social media guru, a dentist and other experts in the community. She was my go-to resource for anything. I mean *anything*. Her advertisers loved her for many reasons, but one of the biggest reasons was her deep network of non-media connections. This was also her differentiating factor. Sure, she was a quality media sales person, but her connections helped her stand a head above the rest in the business. Did it earn her more business? Absolutely.

Here's another quarterly incentive: Once a quarter, you offer to sit down with your IT person and review your advertiser's website traffic for them. Do you know that many business people have no idea how to read their Google analytics? They're clueless. When you provide clients with an opportunity to review their Google analytics with an IT professional, most jump at that offer. Would you charge for that service? Absolutely not. It's an opportunity to build trust and goodwill with your advertisers and a great way to say thank you.

How about offering a Readex Research study to your advertiser? If you don't already know, Readex Research is a great company, which has been around since 1947. They conduct services like ad effectiveness surveys or reader research that could be invaluable to your advertiser.

Yet another great idea for your quarterly incentive is to provide an email survey for your advertiser to find out more about their customers... your readers.. Once a quarter, offer to survey to a select group of your readers on behalf of your advertiser. Ask your advertiser this, "If we could ask your customers one or two questions for you, what would those questions be? This is a great service, and the advertisers always appreciate your effort. And, you get the added benefit of collecting the data, which you can use to your benefit.

Once a quarter, your sales manager should be calling every advertiser. If you spread it out over the year, the task is easily manageable. If you're a sales manager like me, you are paid upon the success of your team. So this is something really important for you to do. I know many sales managers who absolutely refuse to do this. Why? They don't want to give an advertiser an opportunity to complain. Think about it though. What happens to an advertiser who keeps their feelings pent up? Eventually when their contract is up, they're gone. And when an advertiser is upset, how many people will they tell? Experts say a disgruntled customer will tell fifteen other people about their dissatisfaction. On the other hand, happy customers may tell one or two other people. Happy customers are good customers and you can keep them for the long-term. What about lunch with your advertisers? Or lunch with you, your sales manager and the advertiser. Is that something that you can afford to do? Maybe it's something you can't afford NOT to do.

Some of my ideas are better suited for advertisers in a local market. How about those of you who work in a national market? Do it the old fashioned way – pick up your phone and call. Plan a 'lunch and learn' during a trade show when you know your advertisers will be in attendance. Never miss a chance when you are in their area to pay them a non-sales visit and take them to lunch or out for a beverage after work.

Let's not forget our fabulous technology. Schedule a WebEx or GoToMeeting session and offer some of these services as webinars. Everything I've shared with you that happens on a local level can happen on a national level as well. The question is, what quarterly initiatives are you going to use to retain your advertisers? I'm going to bet that most of you do not have a quarterly advertiser retention plan in place......yet.

Retention Plan Focus Area #3: Yearly Initiatives

Let's move to your yearly advertiser incentive plan. Schedule and conduct an annual media-planning meeting where you actually sit down with your advertisers and work with them to plan their advertising goals for the year. I'll even include media buys from my competition. I've done this for years and my advertisers are always surprised – and apprecia-tive. *"Ryan, why would you include media buys from your competition?"* you ask. Because, I want my advertisers to un-derstand that I truly have their best interests in mind. Their success becomes my success.   Of course, I always work to make sure the majority of their media buys are coming my way. (wink)

Another yearly initiative should be to recommend an offer for an annual website review by your IT team for your advertisers website(s). Or, bring in a local partner who can of-fer some thoughtful advice. You could spend $1,000 for a web-site expert and set up a phone conference with six of your top advertisers to go through their websites and offer advice. Your advertisers would love it.

Once a year, offer your customers a cyber security re-view. You can contact almost any IT company that will run security scans on any given website and provide a detailed report of their findings. What would your advertisers think if you offered them that service annually? They would think, "*Wow. That's incredible.*" It's not a lot of money, but it offers a tremendous service to your advertisers and it helps to underscore your worth as a resource to them.

You can also plan an annual advertisers event if you're in a local market. Who doesn't like a party where like-minded people can mingle and enjoy getting to know their peers? You want to make this event as big as you can afford. I often recommend that you spend $10-15k and bring in a dynamic keynote speaker that will draw a crowd. If you're at a national level, plan a reception during a conference where your advertisers are attending. It's about networking and connecting with your advertisers. People like to do business with people who bring business to them. If you network and help advertisers grow their business, you are their hero. Who doesn't love a hero?

Think of initiatives that your company could offer. Once a year, you could offer rate protection to your advertisers. Or maybe you offer a phone call from the publisher or station manager! Or even lunch with the editor and yourself.

And don't forget about the yearly 'bonus bucks' redemption I mentioned earlier.

Finally, as part of your advertiser retention plan, you need a strong referral program. First and foremost, you need something that is easy for your advertisers to understand. Secondly, it is very important that you have a good referral program – 5% off 10% off - is not enough. The referral discount needs to be substantial if you hope to get an advertiser excited enough to share your media referral with their other friends or colleagues in an effort to do business with you. I always tell my clients that they need to create a referral program that if it worked correctly, would allow an advertiser to refer enough business to you that they would get all their advertising free for one year. You want advertisers to know that you are serious about serious referrals. You need to give them something substantial. Call it a loss leader if you want, but you've got to have a referral program that's so strong and so easy for someone to understand that they'll actually spread the word for you. Just imagine an army of advertisers out there talking about you and your products in a very positive way.

So how do you get the message out about your referral program with BIG payouts for your advertisers? Maybe you use printed post card type mailers that are easy to use and easy for you to track. Maybe you try a program where both the referrer and the referee get something out of it. Perhaps a "most referrals per quarter" offers some kind of bonus.

The way that most referral programs work is that an advertiser receives a referral bonus if the client that they referred signs up for a certain amount of advertising. So they are not rewarded just for referring the business. The new advertiser that was referred has to sign a deal with you in order for the referring advertiser to claim their rewards.

If I sound like I'm preaching at you, I'm not—but you really need an advertiser retention plan. My goal is to help you succeed. The media companies that I work with that are a raging success have in place and utilize an active advertiser retention plan. As a matter of fact, some of these companies have employees dedicated to managing their advertiser retention plan. That's how important this process is.

If you don't have an advertiser retention plan, develop one. Immediately. Use a white board and map it out. Don't become guilty of paralysis by analysis. Don't think about this for 15 years and then decide to make this happen overnight. If you only start with small things, that's fine, and you can build on the program continually.

There are dozens of other annual incentive actions that could benefit your retention program, and you can undoubtedly come up with some of your own ideas. Kick it around with your peers and do a little brainstorming — you may amaze yourselves with your innovation and creativity. The point is to develop and implement an advertiser retention program. It is mission critical to your success as an ad sales rep. Do not think that your advertisers are above being rewarded. Everyone likes to get "stuff". And advertisers love to be thanked. Very rarely will you be accused of being a person who thanks clients too much.

If you're a sales manager, a publisher, a GM, an owner, etc. it is really important to get your entire sales team involved from day one on this retention idea. The last thing a sales person wants is for you to give them something else to do. They would much rather be out selling, which is what you really want them to do anyway. So again, when you're putting together an advertiser retention plan, gather together all of your sales team. Bring them together in a conference room — serve them pizza, and get their input and their buy-in on an advertiser retention plan. Help them understand that, as a group, they must decrease attrition and keep the current advertisers on board and very happy.

You know what is really surprising to me? Some of you don't actually know how many advertisers you lose each year. The excuses are many; it must be the economy; sales are just down this year; it must be Obma-care; it's just a sales cycle. The truth is, it often comes down to you and what you do (or do not do) on a regular basis to take care of the advertisers you have. You must prove to your advertisers that you deliver on what you promise and so much more. One you get rid of the excuses you will find the results.

Most advertisers think sales people are a colossal waste of time. Most advertisers only believe that a sales person is there to sell them something. Why do I get so much repeat media business? Because I go out of my way to take care of my customers. I send them things. I give them access to information. I do everything I can think of doing to convince them that I'm a valuable resource that they simply cannot do without. I know how unbelievably important it is to take care of my customers. So if you're expecting your advertisers to track their own success, I have some swamp land to sell you at a really great price. You simply must take care of your advertisers. Obvious? Yes. Often ignored? Yes. Acceptable? No.

CHAPTER EIGHT

Creating your action plan for success.

L et's bring this train back into the station after this journey together. So, what will it take for you to max out your sales after reading this book? First, you need to recognize that you must sell from a new angle or direction if you want to be a raging sales success. For me, writing *Selling Backwards* is all about starting with the advertiser and not with perfecting my pitch. Everything you do with your new approach has to be from a new angle. For me, it was a complete 180. It is all about fulfilling the selfish needs of my advertisers and has almost nothing to do with the media I am selling. It is all about THEM!

There is success that is waiting for you, but I know it's not because of me. This is really what this action plan chapter is about. Skip this last, important step and you will never see the results I know you can achieve.

This book is about providing you with some tools and tips so you can utilize them to become the very best ad sales rep you can possibly be. Now the ball is in your court. You are going to need to dribble that ball to the basket and make the shot for the winning point in the game. You are going to have to make all the moves. All I have done is provide some coaching advice, techniques and processes. It's totally up to YOU to score the points in terms of closing those sales! So this is why an action plan with individual action items is critical to your success working my program.

Here are the seven things I want you to think about when you're building your action plan for success. We will review them in detail in this final chapter together.

Action item #1. Focus on just 5 areas you want to improve.

Action Item #2. Set priorities and dates.

Action Item #3. Find and utilize an accountability buddy.

Action Item #4. Recognize reality.

Action Item# 5. Do NOT give up.

Action Item #6. Do you need help?

Action Item #7. Recognize and accept the challenge.

Before we address your last step in my *Selling Back-wards Sales Process*, I want to thank you for embarking on this journey with me by reading my book, hiring me to come to your office, supporting me at national events each year and watching my 360 Ad Sales videos. I'd like to share a couple of success stories with you. As your prepare your action plan for success, you should know there are many others out there just like you who are having some awesome success following the *Selling Backwards Sales Process*.

Not long ago I finished working with Gina, a sales executive for a city and regional magazine in Texas. When I showed up for our workshop together, I could tell Gina was just down on herself and down on her product. She said, *"Ryan, I've tried every method, read every sales book and downloaded every DVD I could get my hands on. Nothing is working for me!"* I asked several questions and quickly determined that the sales advice she had been following was generic sales training at best. But, more importantly, Gina lacked a plan to identify repeatable patterns of success. In addition, she did not have a plan to execute what she was learning on a daily basis. I asked for her faith and asked her to try my methods, which were created specifically for ad sales. I asked Gina to at least work my *Big 50 Prospecting Plan* for thirty days and she agreed.

I recently received an email from this Gina, which said, *"Ryan, thank you SO much for sharing the Selling Backwards Sales Process with me. My sales have grown 35% and I have been offered the job of sales manager at my company."* I love stories like this!

A very good friend of mine, Doug, is one of my favorite examples of success. Doug followed my *Selling Backwards Sales Process* to a tee. Every day. For 2 years! His sales grew over 125%. Then, Doug was recruited by a very large newspaper and is now their sales manager earning well over six-figures a year. Stories like Gina and Doug are very meaningful to me. It tells me the processes I spent so much time perfecting are being used by people quite successfully.

Ok, so now the "real work" begins. Let's dig in.

Action item #1. Focus on just 5 areas in your sales life that you want to improve. Don't try to do 10 or 15 things – it can't be done. You are just too busy. Stick to 5 items you wish to improve. Here are some examples. If you know you're not very good at prospecting, make that one area of your five and use my *Big 50 Prospecting Plan*. Of course, within that process, there are several steps; creating templates, practicing, etc., Maybe you need work on one of the steps within the process. If prospecting isn't your weak area then maybe you just need practice hosting great sales calls. Make that one of your items. Review your notes, look back through this book, study a couple of my videos again. Make my sales processes work for you. Identify the five areas that are holding you back from higher sales success.

Action Item #2. Set priorities and dates.

Once you've identified your 5 areas of improvement, go back through the list and prioritize. I recommend that you tackle the most difficult task first. Why? Because after reading this book you will have a certain level of inspiration and excitement that will fade with time. Then assign realistic dates to each of the five items. What you don't want to do is to start working on it every Monday at 9 am. Realistically, that is not going to work. You need to allow yourself fourteen to seventeen days for each action item to be completed. You might be thinking, *"Ryan, that time frame is not going to work either, because I need to fix my process right* now!" Well, I'm one of those impatient people too. I want it all yesterday! Or you might be thinking, *"Man, I've kids at home, I'm in the middle of building a house, (etc. etc.) I just don't have time to work on five areas of improvement."* No matter the roadblocks, simply assign dates for each of your five and make the dates as realistic as possible given your own personal work habits and outside responsibilities.

Action Item #3. Find and utilize an accountability buddy.

When do you tend to lose the most weight? You lose the most weight when you have a partner or an accountability buddy – someone who is going to keep you on task. When do you exercise the most? When you're working out with a partner or trainer. Similarly, find someone who will follow up with you and help you monitor your progress. You can hire a professional coach, use your sales manager or ask a peer you respect. You can even use Outlook to send you reminders of your tasks.

Action Item #4. Recognize reality.

It is critical to recognize that it's going to take between 17 and 20 days for you to form a new habit. Experts sometimes debate the number of days required to acquire a new habit and of course the number of days will vary depending on the individual. (It will usually take me almost a month to lock in a new sales habit!) So you have to remember that when you are making phone calls, use your *Big 50* templates. If you are trying to sell with a pricing grid, don't go out on two, three, four or even five sales calls and expect that's it's going to take off immediately like wild fire. New habits can be formed, but they won't become permanent behavior patterns without a lot of repetition and commitment over time. Practice, practice and more practice. You will not get to play at Carnegie Hall after only seven days of piano lessons.

Action Item # 5. Do NOT give up.

Why is this an actual action item? Because it is very important to remember that a lot of the ad sales processes I've covered are going to work better on <u>new </u>advertisers. You have probably either ruined many of your old advertisers or you have spoiled a lot of them. So when you're building this action plan, remember this tip—*plan forward and don't give up.*

Action Item #6. Do you need help?

You may need to consider finding a mentor or getting a sales coach. This is not a sales pitch for my services. There are a lot of coaches out there who can help you. It might even be your sales manager, yoru GM, Your publisher, your companies owner, etc. It might be someone you know from the Rotary club, or Chamber of Commerce. It might even be one of your trusted advertisers. At the very least subscribe to my e-newsletters, or check out motivational leaders like Tony Robbins, or other coaches who specialize in personal growth. There are so many people out there whom you can learn from to improve your sales life.

There are also a ton of life coaches available. Many people don't recognize the power a life coach can have on your long term personal and business success. A coach is going to listen to you, provide thoughtful ideas and hold you accountable. There are a ton of reasons to utilize a coach, and they are all good.

Action Item #7. Recognize and accept the challenge.

No matter how you say it—you are the quarterback. The buck stops with you. You are the pilot of your plane. I've tried to give you the tools you'll need and shared success stories with you. Recognize that it's all up to you. You are the one who has to make the decisions. You control your destiny. Your success is not by chance, it is by choice. If you want better success in your sales life, the only way you are going to improve is to first recognize that you have a problem. Then you can begin to fix the problems. By working the *Selling Backwards Sales Process*, you can achieve your goals.

Some of you reading this may be superstars already. You're awesome! So let's go from superstar to extraterrestrial! For you, greater sales success is about merely tweaking a process and then repeatedly executing it.

Some of you will watch my videos and read this book and say, *"Well Ryan, that was a nice little refresher – those were all things I heard before. I see now that I need to put them in action."* Once you get rid of the excuses you will find results.

1. Identify 5 items for improvement that you can absolutely sink your teeth into.

2. Put dates on those items and put them on your calendar with realistic deadlines.

3. Get an accountability buddy. You will need help to stay on track. Trust me on this point.

4. Recognize that it will take some time to form a new habit.

5. Don't give up. This new process takes time to develop and time to implement. You are NOT going to go from $10,000 one week to $200,000 the next. Not going to happen!

6. Look to hire a coach or a mentor. Find someone who is willing to give you constructive criticism.

7. Recognize and accept that the ball is in your court, all 100%.

Here's the last lesson I'll share with you. There is a wonderful gentleman who came into my career life at an early age. His name is Billy Morris, and he's a publisher, an outdoorsman, a horseman and a serial entrepreneur. Mr. Morris came into my life because he purchased websites from my wife and I and then brought me into his publishing business in Augusta, GA.

I had some publishing experience prior to meeting Mr. Morris, but he brought me in at a time when the Internet was in its infancy. The best thing Mr. Morris did for me was to say, *"Ryan, I believe in you, I'm going to give you an investment so you can make your ideas happen and guess what – the ball is in your court. So, make it happen."*

With Billy Morris' encouragement and leadership, I earned my MBA in Publishing and Ad Sales while with his company. I left him in 2008 and then went on to create the 360 Ad Sales System, a ton of ad sales training videos and have been blessed with the opportunity to coach business clients and sale people all over the world. And now I've written *Selling Back-wards* as a way to take my ad sales training to the next level for all of you. I sincerely hope this book helps you to become successful beyond your wildest dreams.

So, the ball is in your court... start dribbling! And remember...if ad sales were easy, everyone would be doing it!

More online at www.360AdSales.com

This is an fictional example of the sales sheet that I refer to as my data sheet/ audience profile.

OUR READERS ARE **Business Owners & Executives**

We are read by 85,000 affluent business owners and executives!

That is more people than you could fit in Ohio Stadium on any given Saturday!

Total Readers: 85,000
Average Age: 42
Family size: 4
Household Income: $275k
$45k per year spent on home improvement.
$35k per year on private school.
2 nights per week dining out.
3500 Facebook Likes
3200 Twitter Followers
35,000 unique readers to our website each month.

This is a concept sample using fictional data and images. J Bryan Swell Media 2014

This is a fictional example of the sales sheet that I would use to showcase all of my media offerings. I call this my multi-media offerings one sheet.

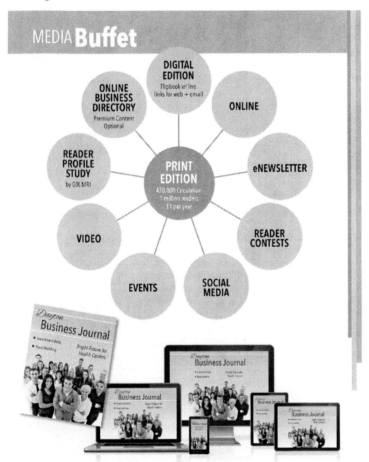

This is an example of a pricing grid that showcases all you get when you buy multi-media from me. Thanks Esther and Andrea for your faith in my systems.

Metropolitan
www.barcelona-metropolitan.com

Call us on +34 93 451 4486 to learn how we've been showing real results to our clients for over 18 years.

Choose any of our multimedia packages and we will create the campaign to your specific needs.

EXPAND YOUR VISIBILITY WITH A MULTIMEDIA CAMPAIGN

Affordable packages for YOUR MARKETING campaign

CHOOSE YOUR PACKAGE ←	MAGAZINE	ONLINE DIRECTORY	SOCIAL MEDIA	WEB BANNER	NEWSLETTER
SMALL BUSINESS Annual total value £2636 Price with discount £1476 Saving £1160 From £123/month	✓	✓	✓		
VISIBILITY Annual total value £4662 Price with discount £2604 Saving £2048 From £217/month	✓	✓	✓	✓	
BRAND RECOGNITION Annual total value £9206 Price with discount £5208 Saving £4098 From £434/month	✓	✓	✓	✓	✓

Creative Media Group, Gran 7 2-4 08002 Barcelona Tel 93 451 4486, info@barcelona-metropolitan.com

ABOUT THE AUTHOR

Ryan Dohrn is the founder of media sales consulting firm Brain Swell Media and the creator of the 360 Ad Sales System taught to over 3,000 ad sales around the globe. Ryan has been a sales and marketing leader for the NY Times Company, Cumulus Radio, Disney-ABC TV, Sinclair Broadcasting and Morris Magazines. He has been featured in USA Today on CNN Radio and on Forbes.com. Ryan currently works on a monthly basis with over 75 media companies and their related sales and management teams.

Lightning Source UK Ltd.
Milton Keynes UK
UKOW02f0704021216
288932UK00003B/263/P